solutions

hamlyn

meditation solutions

Paul Roland

Guided meditations for health and peace of mind

This book is affectionately dedicated to
Noreen Emmans, counsellor, teacher and
friend, for generously sharing her insights
into the human condition.

First published in Great Britain in 2002 by
Hamlyn, a division of
Octopus Publishing Group Ltd
2–4 Heron Quays, London E14 4JP

Copyright © Octopus Publishing
Group Ltd 2002

ISBN 0 600 60483 7

A CIP catalogue record for this book is available
from the British Library

Printed and bound in China

10 9 8 7 6 5 4 3 2 1

Disclaimer

The meditation and visualization exercises included in this book
are designed for relaxation and for developing self-awareness.
However, anyone who has emotional or mental problems, or
who has had problems of this nature in the past, should seek
professional medical advice before attempting any of these
exercises. The author and the publisher accept no
responsibility for any harm caused by or to anyone as a result
of the misuse of these exercises.

Contents

Introduction

This book is not just another course describing the many benefits and techniques of meditation, but a menu consisting of over 100 original exercises for exploring, understanding and improving specific aspects of mind, body and spirit. The exercises employ both visualizations and affirmations. In the first, the imagination is used to imprint an image on the unconscious, and, in the second, positive assertions are imprinted while in the meditative state. It is aimed at people with busy, stressful lives who are looking for an effective method of relaxation, and also for those who wish to develop their self-awareness. The meditations should take between 10 and 30 minutes – 10 for the basic ones, 20 for the average, and 30 for the most complex. It is not advisable to spend more than 30 minutes each day in meditation, otherwise you risk becoming a 'bliss junkie', ignoring your responsibilities and putting your relationships at risk.

What is meditation?

Whenever we become completely absorbed in an activity involving either physical effort or passive contemplation, we enter an altered state of consciousness similar to that sought in meditation. Yet, at such times, the sense of detachment and heightened concentration is not sustained for long enough to produce a lasting effect. Meditation is the process of deliberately entering this altered state. When practised on a regular basis for 10–20 minutes a day, it can have a profound effect on our mental and emotional well-being, as well as improving and maintaining our physical health.

Meditation has been proven to have a significant therapeutic effect on certain physical and mental conditions. Its potential for enhancing self-awareness and promoting personal growth, however, is limitless. In its more advanced forms, it can help alter one's state of awareness, from the self-centred perspective of the physical world through an exploration of the symbolic landscape of the psyche to an acute awareness of the greater reality of which we are all a part.

Waking consciousness

This is our normal, everyday awareness of the physical dimension, the point from which we start a meditation and to which we return at the end, usually by counting down from ten to one. It may also be necessary to stamp our feet in order to 'ground' ourselves properly in the physical world.

What this book covers

The first section, Health and Healing, begins with basic breath control, mindfulness and visualization exercises for increasing body awareness, conserving energy, healing, revitalizing and deep relaxation. Then it goes deeper, describing more advanced techniques for self-diagnosis of the most common physical ailments, simple visualizations for pain relief and a script for self-hypnosis to alleviate psychosomatic symptoms and sleep disorders.

The second section, Emotions, includes exercises for overcoming nerves, getting a grip on fears and phobias, coming to terms with loss and channelling anger and hostility into creative energy. It concludes with several tried and tested techniques for improving relationships and letting go of emotional ties. These exercises suggest that if we illuminate our shadow self and face our fears we will become more authentic, complete and mature individuals, in control of our lives rather than at the mercy of circumstances.

'The life which is unexamined is not worth living.'

Plato
Dialogues

The third section, Mind Matters, describes various visualizations for stress relief, increasing self-awareness, strengthening self-confidence, creating abundance, dispelling depression, dealing with addiction and resolving issues such as guilt, negative conditioning and forgiveness. The more you work with these techniques the more you will feel in control of your own life and the more confident you will become in being able to resolve your own issues.

The fourth section, Soul Searching, reveals the potential of meditation for probing the depths of the unconscious and seeking guidance from the Higher Self. It also includes visualizations for creating an inner sanctuary, exploring the symbolic landscape of the psyche and empowering the various complementary aspects of the personality, before offering a glimpse of the greater reality that will ultimately lead to enlightenment.

1 Health and healing

Basic breath control for conserving energy

We tend to think of breathing as an automatic function that does not require any thought or conscious control, but the manner in which we breathe can determine our emotional response to stressful situations, our energy levels and even our general health. When we sleep or enter into a state of deep relaxation we drop down a gear, so to speak, breathing from the diaphragm, the muscular membrane that lies between the chest and abdominal cavities. When we are active, however, we take shallow breaths from the chest, which restricts the flow of oxygen to the lungs, creating a sense of anxiety and tension and also inhibiting the release of toxins which can poison the system. The following exercises will help you become aware of how you are breathing.

Breathing from the diaphragm

Lie on your back with one hand on your chest and the other on your stomach.

Inhale while pushing your stomach out and exhale while drawing your stomach in. The hand that is on your chest should remain still. Breathing in this way automatically creates a sense of tranquillity and makes it difficult to indulge in negative emotions associated with a tension in the chest.

Now remove the hand from your stomach and breathe from your chest. Does this remind you of the way you feel when you are stressed or nervous?

feel the essence of your being expanding to fill the room . . .

'Whatever you can do, or dream you can, begin it. Boldness has genius, magic and power in it. Begin it now.'

Goethe

Breathing in the universal life force

This technique is simple but surprisingly effective. Sit with your back straight and take a deep breath from the diaphragm, as you did before, but this time draw the air from your diaphragm up into your chest and then further up into your lungs.

Establish a regular rhythm of breathing in and out, which should be slightly deeper than the way you breathe naturally, but it should never be laboured. You could try using a counting system (see page 49).

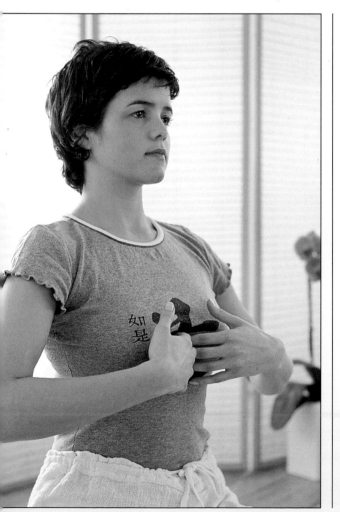

As you breathe in, imagine that you are inhaling the universal life force (see page 123) in the form of a radiant white light. Know that there is no limit to how much of this vital energy you can consume. It permeates your skin, your muscles and even your bones, saturating and revitalizing every cell of your being.

You now radiate energy like a sun. Feel the essence of your being expanding to fill the room with light as this infusion of energy stimulates the chakras (see page 16), which are the vortices of etheric energy at key points in the body. As these vortices spin, they release etheric energy which can be visualized as coloured light radiating outwards to form the aura, a multicoloured corona of light around the body. Keep this image in your mind for as long as you can, and enjoy the sense of unlimited energy that it creates.

When you are ready, close down and seal the energy within by running your hands from the crown of your head to your toes as if smoothing the energy field that now surrounds you. When you feel ready to return to waking consciousness, open your eyes and stamp your feet to ground yourself in the physical world.

Grounding meditation

One of the few possible negative 'side-effects' of meditation is that its pleasant sense of detachment can become addictive. For this reason, it is advisable for beginners to limit their exercises to between 20 and 30 minutes and include a grounding visualization such as the one described here, three to four times a week, to keep in contact with the physical world.

feel the power and majesty of the oak · · ·

Preparation

I have set this visualization on a warm summer's afternoon, but you can vary the setting to another season or time of day if you wish. Such minor details can have a subtle but profound effect on the unconscious, altering the quality and nature of the experience. For example, you might find that imagining a moonlit autumn scene brings a greater sense of serenity and peace of mind, which might be beneficial if you are doing the exercise before going to sleep, whereas a crisp winter morning scene might prove more invigorating and therefore ideal for starting your day. In contrast, a spring scene can encourage a more positive outlook and prove fertile ground for new ideas, while summer helps to create an atmosphere of deep relaxation.

Make yourself comfortable in a straight-backed chair or armchair and begin by focusing on the breath.

Using your imagination

Relax into this visualization by imagining that you are seated on a soft grassy mound overlooking an unspoilt view of rolling hills and fields. Your back rests against the trunk of a massive oak tree, whose leaves shade you from the warmth of the sun. Snuggle into the trunk, which supports you, and begin to get a sense of the size and strength of this imposing oak.

As you drift into deeper relaxation, you lose your sense of self and become as one with this living manifestation of nature.

Visualize your legs intertwining with the enormous roots stretching deep into the earth, securing the trunk to the ground. Know that no storm could tear it from the soil. It has stood firm for a century and will stand for many more, drawing strength from deep within the earth, as you do now.

Now imagine stretching your arms to the sky, and see these too becoming blurred as they merge with the branches that are reaching heavenward.

Feel the power and majesty of the oak stretching towards the sun, and drawing the power of sunlight down to feed the leaves which rustle gently in the breeze. Soak up the sunlight into every cell of your being, and sense it melting into the energy you are drawing up from the earth. Feel the power, strength and security that being a channel for the celestial and terrestrial forces gives you.

When you are ready, sense the weight of your body resting against the trunk of the tree, and then return to waking consciousness by counting slowly down from ten to one.

After opening your eyes, stamp your feet to reaffirm your contact with the physical world.

'Your body is the ground and metaphor of your life, the expression of your existence . . . in the marriage of flesh and spirit divorce is impossible.'

Gabrielle Roth

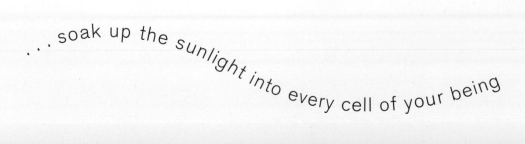
. . . soak up the sunlight into every cell of your being

Deep relaxation

When practising visualizations, it is usually enough to make yourself comfortable, closing your eyes and focusing on the breath, knowing that the body will relax as your conscious mind becomes detached from the physical world. If, however, you need deep physical relaxation to alleviate stress or physical ailments, you will have to become more in tune with your body and acutely aware of the mind's capacity for transferring tension to parts of the body.

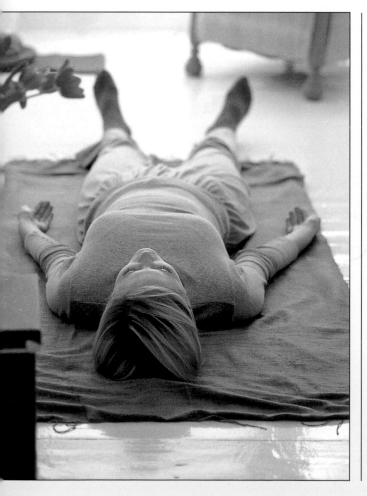

Bodyscanning

This is a good exercise to do both in bed at night before drifting off to sleep and first thing in the morning to tone you up for the day. It should be performed lying down with your arms loose by your sides and your feet slightly apart. Alternatively, if you think there might be an emotional blockage to be dissolved, cup your hands together beneath the navel to focus energy at the solar plexus.

When you are relaxed and breathing in a regular rhythm, focus your attention on your toes. Do not just *think* about your toes, but try to shift your whole awareness to that area of your body.

This projection of consciousness is one of the most difficult disciplines to master, but it is also one of the most important. It will help you to target a particular area of the body more effectively when you are healing yourself or another person, and you will also find it easier to let go of many negative thoughts that might otherwise manifest as the physical symptoms of dis-ease (a state of imbalance in the psyche).

visualize yourself giving a perfect performance . . .

'If you don't take care of your body, where will you live?'

Anonymous

Now curl your toes and hold that position for a moment before relaxing.

Continue this systematic tensing and relaxing technique all the way up your body, paying particular attention to your lower back, shoulders and face. Take your time and be thorough in giving your full attention to every muscle that can be moved.

Tensing each part in this way acknowledges the subtle stresses in the body of which we are often unconscious, but which combine to put a serious and sustained strain on our system.

Visualization

This exercise is very simple, but you should make it last at least ten minutes to get the full benefit and to impress the imagery on the unconscious.

Make yourself comfortable and become aware of the weight and warmth of your body. Imagine yourself at the centre of this highly complex human creature that is strong and agile.

Now visualize yourself performing your daily tasks or something that you wish to improve upon, such as playing sport or practising a musical instrument. Observe your body movements, noting your posture and any unnecessary strain that could be inhibiting your performance.

Then visualize yourself giving a perfect performance and sense the pride and pleasure this gives you. Imprint this image on your body consciousness by imagining that you are filming the performance for posterity and tell yourself that this is how it should be done and that you will do it this way, effortlessly, every time from now on.

Increasing body awareness

An increasing number of people in the west are beginning to accept a concept shared by many esoteric traditions and the eastern philosophies, which envisage the physical body as an external shell within which is a second form of finer matter commonly known as the etheric, emotional or astral body. This matrix of energy forms the framework for its physical counterpart, animating the skeletal structure and muscles so that our essence – pure consciousness – can operate in and experience the physical world. This exercise is designed to heighten your awareness of this multidimensional aspect of your being and to introduce the chakras – the key energy centres.

The body of energy

When you have established a regular rhythm of breathing, externalize your point of view by visualizing yourself, sitting in a chair or lying down, from the other side of the room. As you observe your body from this objective perspective, see it being gradually drained of colour and substance, leaving your body looking like a glass mannequin.

Standing outside this transparent figure, you observe the seven vortices of energy spinning at the Crown Chakra above the head, the Brow or Third Eye Chakra in the middle of the forehead, the Throat Chakra, the Heart Chakra in the middle of the chest, the Solar Plexus Chakra at the stomach, the Sacral Chakra just below the navel, and the Root Chakra at the base of the spine. Each chakra has a corresponding colour: Crown (white), Brow or Third Eye (violet), Throat (blue), Heart (green), Solar Plexus (yellow), Sacral (red) and Root (brown).

Now return your awareness to your body and imagine a network of vein-like lines connecting the vortices to each other and to the muscles and vital organs. These are the meridians that circulate the life force. Sense the chakras spinning, maintaining the balance of energy that keeps you centred and ensuring that the body's organs function efficiently. Next, sense the life force circulating through the meridian lines, sustaining the body's defences and revitalizing every cell.

Be aware that your body is a living, self-regenerating structure sustained by the life force whose power has no limit, and that you have access to this power at all times for healing, understanding and creativity.

'Abide at the centre of your being, for the more you leave it, the less you learn.'

Tao Te Ching

The four elements

You can heighten your awareness of the constituent elements of the physical body by contemplating each in turn.

Begin by focusing on the breath, considering as you do so that this is the air element of your physical body. A heightened awareness of the breath ensures the free circulation of prana, or universal energy, and physical well-being.

Next visualize the blood circulating in your veins, carrying oxygen to the vital organs and antibodies to fight infection. Consider this as the water element of your physical form.

Now sense the heat in your skin, which maintains the temperature of the body, and consider this as the fire element of your physical being.

Finally, focus on the skeletal structure which supports you and gives your body form. Consider this as the mineral or earth element.

Extend your awareness into the outside world and contemplate how these elements work within nature to sustain the cycle of life on Earth.

When you are ready, return to waking consciousness, but try to sustain this heightened awareness of the interrelated nature of things in your everyday life.

Healing

Meditation is commonly considered to be a means of quietening the mind for peace and relaxation, but it can also heal the body by channelling the universal life force to the source of the dis-ease. The life force stimulates the body's own defences to fight the infection and revitalize the cells. It restores the natural balance of the body, while avoiding the possibility of unpleasant side-effects associated with medication. The following visualization impresses a positive image on the unconscious to maintain a state of good health all year round.

Spiritual sunbathing

Visualize a sphere of radiant white light above your head. Become aware of its warmth, vibrant energy and healing properties.

Now draw it in through the crown of your head and visualize its radiance illuminating you from within. Absorb the warmth and energy into every pore of your skin, every muscle fibre, tissue, organ, bone, blood vessel and cell as it saturates your body from crown to toe in the universal life force.

Envisage the light radiating outwards through every pore to bathe you in an aura of revitalizing energy, making you impervious to infection.

Affirm, or assert positively, to yourself that you are in perfect health and will always be so. Take as much time as you like to enjoy this method of spiritual

'In everyday life pain is inevitable, but suffering is optional.'

Dan Millman
Everyday Enlightenment

sunbathing. On waking, try to sustain the all-pervading sense of power and peace you have tapped into for the rest of the day.

Laser treatment

To treat a specific injury, infection or a tumour, use this variation on the spiritual sunbathing exercise as many times a day as you wish.

Begin with the spiritual sunbathing visualization, but, instead of returning to waking consciousness after the affirmation, imagine that a second sphere of light appears above your head. Draw it in as before and when it reaches your Brow Chakra see it intensify into a beam of brilliant white light like a laser.

Now direct it to the source of the infection, to the tumour, to the strained muscle or to the broken bone, and watch as it scans the area, burning away the infected or malignant cells. Watch as they shrivel and disintegrate into the aura like paper in a fire.

Affirm that you are healed and in perfect health, and know that it is so.

Revitalizing

In many spiritual traditions, the use of water in a ritual is more than symbolic. It is believed that water can cleanse the aura of impurities and seal the chakras, ensuring that no one can disturb our equilibrium or penetrate the bubble of sacred space that we can create around ourselves. The following exercise is intended to replicate the effect of ritual cleansing using imagery alone, so that it can be practised at any time, anywhere.

The waterfall

Relax into meditation by focusing on the breath. When you have quietened the mind, visualize yourself standing at the entrance to a forest. Sense the stillness of this place and the peace that awaits you here. You enter, following a track that leads into the heart of the forest where the carpet of leaves is illuminated by shafts of warm sunlight. Feel the softness of the leaves beneath your feet and listen for the sound of small animals rustling through the undergrowth as birds flit from branch to branch overhead.

Soon you can hear the sound of rushing water growing louder as you move towards the centre. In a while, you come upon a clearing framed by the foliage. In the centre of the clearing is a lake, and on the far side a waterfall. There is not a soul in sight.

Take off your soiled clothes and put your toes in the cool, refreshing water. Feel the revitalizing power of nature soaking into the soles of your feet and saturating

'I often compare the mind in meditation to a jar of muddy water: the more we leave the water without interfering or stirring it, the more the particles of dirt will sink to the bottom, letting the natural clarity of the water shine through.'

Sogyal Rinpoche

every cell of your being, as it is absorbed through the skin, into the muscles, even penetrating the bones. The dirt and dust of the everyday world is washed away in an instant, and so are any aches and pains, mental, emotional and physical, that you might have harboured. Now wade out to the far side of the lake and stand beneath the tumbling stream of the waterfall which cleanses every particle of your being. Feel the water gushing down the back of your neck and trickling over your face.

Relax and enjoy the invigorating waters until you are ready to return the way you came.

The pool

When you have entered a deep state of relaxation (see page 14), envisage yourself standing at the entrance to an imposing bathhouse, such as might be found in Rome, Egypt or ancient Greece. You push the massive ornate doors open and step inside. You are quite alone. In the centre of this opulent room is a massive bath filled with steaming water. On the steps leading down into the water can be seen an assortment of bottled ointments of various colours, seven in total, and a neat pile of towels. You step into the water and immediately feel your senses enveloped in a luxurious warmth, releasing the coils of tension that had gripped you.

Now choose one of the coloured bottles and pour the contents into the water, watching as the water changes colour accordingly. Each coloured bottled corresponds to a specific chakra (see pages 36–37), and is capable of revitalizing and restoring energy to each of these subtle centres of the body. Take time to enjoy the water then, when you are ready, return to waking consciousness.

Self-diagnosis

If you are suffering from a recurrent complaint and suspect that the cause might lie with an unresolved issue in your past, or is connected with negative conditioning, it is possible to identify the source of the problem and clear it. The following exercises use a form of meditation that is a cross between creative visualization, pathworking and self-hypnosis.

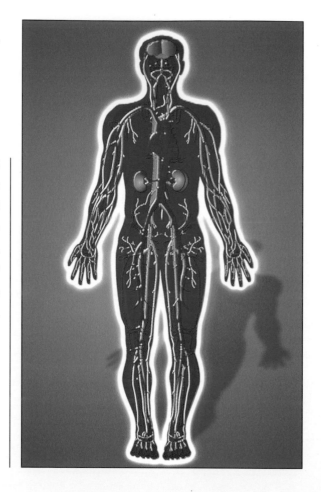

Finding the source of a problem

Lie on your back with your arms by your sides and your feet slightly apart. Close your eyes and establish a regular rhythm of breathing.

When you are in a deep state of relaxation, ask your body to reveal the source of your problem and ask it what the symptoms signify.

Be receptive to whatever comes through and do not dismiss it out of hand as a product of your imagination until you have had a chance to consider it once you have returned to waking consciousness. You may receive an answer immediately in the same way that an idea can spontaneously appear in your mind, or it may appear in symbolic form. It is possible that you may receive an answer in your dreams when the defences of the conscious mind are down. More than likely, however, you will find that an image will appear while you meditate, an image that does not at first seem to be relevant to the question. Do not be tempted to analyse what you see. Simply follow it and let the scene unfold in its own time. All you have to do is remain relaxed, receptive and stay with it as if you are watching a movie.

Entering the scene

You may see a figure somewhere in the picture. This is likely to be your guide. Focus on this person and travel with them through the landscape. If you see a vehicle of some description, project yourself into it and allow yourself to be taken to where the answer awaits you.

Many people find themselves at the entrance to a tunnel. If this happens to you, do not be afraid to enter, even if it is dark. The light will come and you will be able to move through the tunnel with ease. Do not be surprised if you eventually find that the landscape of your imagination has transformed itself into something quite different and that you are now exploring your own body.

You will know when you have reached the end of your journey. There will be no urge to go further, and you should have discovered the answer that you sought, probably in symbolic form. You can ask for the significance of this symbol to be revealed to you, or you can analyse it when you return to waking consciousness.

You have been exploring a very deep level of consciousness and therefore need to emerge from this meditation gradually by counting slowly down from ten to one and becoming aware of your body and your surroundings. Seal your aura by running your hands over your body from crown to toe and stamp your feet to ground yourself.

'All we need to do to receive direct help is to ask . . . and yet, asking is what we find hardest.'

Sogyal Rinpoche

you are now exploring your own body · · ·

Identifying causes of ailments

Those who practise holistic medicine in its many forms assert that the psyche expresses imbalance, infection and dis-ease in 'appropriate' parts of the body, a belief shared by the science of mental health which is founded on the principle that extreme emotions can disrupt the function of the internal organs. By manifesting a skin complaint such as eczema, for example, the body could be drawing attention to an unconscious fear that something unpleasant is 'getting under the patient's skin'. By becoming aware of such signals we can identify the cause of the complaint and treat the source rather than the symptoms. On the following pages, you will find possible explanations for psychosomatic ailments in various parts of the body, together with suggestions for identifying the source of the problem using visualization.

the body could be drawing attention to an unconscious fear . . .

Right side

The right side of the body corresponds to the masculine, active and practical aspect of the psyche. Any ache in this area suggests problems with expressing the masculine aspect of the personality, a lack of confidence, introversion or a fear of change.

Visualization: Imagine a scene in which you are a child being shown how things work by a male mentor whom you admire – a kind and considerate father figure, a favourite uncle, a male teacher or a brother. He listens patiently and answers your questions until your curiosity is satisfied. Know and affirm that his knowledge, confidence, strength and willingness to share his time and wisdom are qualities that you have, too, and that you will manifest in your life.

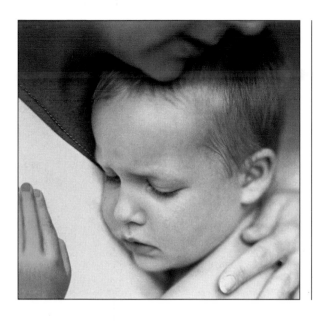

Left side

The left side corresponds to the feminine, passive and intuitive aspect. Difficulties in this area suggest problems with expressing emotions, accepting affection and repressed creative energy.

Visualization: Imagine a scene at night in which you are a small child being comforted by a maternal figure – a mother, a favourite aunt, a teacher or an elder sister. As you look out at the moon in a cloudless sky, you confide in her and she listens to your troubles with compassion, understanding and unconditional love. Now affirm that these qualities are also within you.

Torso

'When you really listen to yourself, you can heal yourself.'

Ceanne Derohan

The region from waist to head contains the energy centres that govern the intellect and emotions. Problems in this area indicate possible difficulties in making decisions, as thoughts can be confused by emotional issues. For example, we might know that it is right for us to move to another town, but we might be held back from doing so by worrying about the family and friends we leave behind.

Visualization: Imagine that you are giving advice to someone in an identical situation to yourself. Listen to their concerns and, if they are worried about how their decision may affect others, imagine that you can also consult the other party. What do they say about it? What advice do you give?

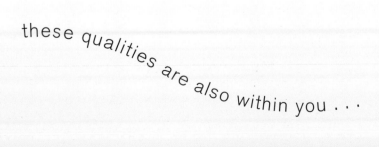

these qualities are also within you . . .

Lower half

The lower half of the body contains the Sacral and Root Chakras, which govern the physical functions such as reproduction, digestion and our connection to the earth. Ailments in this area suggest difficulties with processing energy, assimilating experience and clearing unresolved issues. There might also be resistance to becoming self-sufficient, independent and committed to one specific job, place or relationship.

Visualization: Imagine a scene that emphasizes emotional and physical security and support, such as seeing yourself enjoying your success and having a happy home life.

Back

The lower back is linked to the solar plexus, and can therefore trap repressed emotions, particularly those concerned with resentment. The back can 'lock up' when we fear that we might have to carry too much responsibility or that we might not be able to support ourselves, or when we doubt that we might have the strength to overcome some difficulty.

Visualization: Breathing from the diaphragm (see page 10) should release any tension in the solar plexus and take the strain away from the lower back. A useful visualization is to see yourself pushing an enormous boulder up a steep hill, which becomes smaller and lighter as you approach the summit as the friction grinds it down into a small rock. At the top, it is transformed into a balloon, which you release and watch float away into a cloudless sky.

Bladder

Bladder ailments are often concerned with control issues, fear and the inability to express emotions. Such problems frequently originate in early childhood when the only certain way of receiving parental attention is to urinate.

Visualization: Imagine a scene or situation in which you entrust your future and family to the universal force in the form of an angel or radiant spiritual being who will nurture and sustain you. See yourself and your family enfolded in its wings. Know that, whatever form this force takes, it is as real as anything in the physical dimension and that its unconditional love for you is eternal.

Bowels

Chronic constipation indicates a reluctance to come to terms with unpleasant experiences and to let go of attachments, whereas continual bouts of diarrhoea suggest a rush to get things done without due consideration. Digestive problems, such as irritable bowel syndrome, can be symptomatic of a conflict between the desire to be done with something and a reluctance to let it go. In addition, such problems can indicate an urge to control events that are clearly beyond the influence of the individual.

Visualization: See yourself on a mountain peak as a storm gathers strength in the distance. Watch as it rips through the valley below, whipping up dust clouds but doing little material damage. You are unable to control the elemental forces, but you are not afraid. There is no consciousness at the centre of the storm. There is nothing intent on causing harm. Affirm that this, too, will pass. Now watch as the storm abates and the inhabitants emerge in the early morning light to patiently repair the damage and continue life as before.

Breasts

It has been suggested that some cases of breast cancer may originate with, or are exacerbated by, emotional problems concerned with motherhood, such as anxiety about being a 'good' mother or guilt.

Visualization: Try the meditations suggested for guilt (see page 92), healing (see page 18) and the left side of the body (see page 25).

Ears

If ear infections and hearing impairments are psychosomatic in origin, it could be that there is an unconscious desire to 'turn a deaf ear' to the truth of a situation or be unreceptive to the opinion of others.

Visualization: Imagine that you have a pulsating sphere of universal energy in each palm and that you can direct this light to your fingertips. Visualize putting a finger to the affected ear and see the light enter and be absorbed into the skin. Sense the warmth of the healing energy as it dissolves the blockage and regenerates the affected cells.

Eyes

Difficulties with eyesight can be caused by an unconscious desire to filter out unpleasantness and withdraw into oneself so as not to have to face reality. As previously stated, these comments apply only to psychosomatic disorders. If you have any serious physical symptoms you should consult your doctor.

Visualization: Imagine that you are sitting in complete darkness and that you can hear the faint sound of summer outside your room. The unmistakable sounds of lawns being mown, birds singing and the buzz of insects drift through an open window. The curtains are drawn slightly and a shaft of sunlight warms your face. The urge to draw the curtains open fully and go into the garden on such a beautiful warm day is overwhelming. Go to the window, draw the curtains aside and, when your eyes have become accustomed to the dazzling light, go out through the patio door. Explore the garden and affirm that you will never close your eyes or your senses to beauty again.

Feet and legs

On a purely symbolic level, problems in the legs and feet would seem to suggest worries about being able to support oneself (to 'stand on one's own two feet'), or it might signify a reluctance to move on to a new situation. It could also indicate a purely physical problem, however, such as poor circulation. In either case, meditation can be beneficial.

Visualization: When you have entered a deep state of relaxation, imagine that you can step outside of yourself, leaving the physical body behind sitting in the chair. Watch your 'spirit double' leave the room, go out of the house and down the street. As it moves further away, it becomes lighter, losing all feeling in the legs and feet as it walks on the air. Rising above the town, it looks down and you can observe through its eyes people going about their business. Everyone has their responsibilities and you feel drawn to play your part, knowing that the universal life force is with you literally every step of the way. Sense how liberated you feel when freed from the physical shell, and affirm that you are ready to take the first steps towards a horizon of infinite possibilities. Know that now nothing can hold you back.

Genitals

The genitals are very sensitive to nervous disorders, and as such can be the focus of a wide range of emotional problems such as inhibitions, feelings of vulnerability and guilt.

Visualization: Imagine that you are seated opposite a full-length mirror in which you can see your reflection. Become aware that it is your reflection that goes out into the world, the world of the mirror, while the real you remains here calm and centred. Watch with detachment as your reflection reacts to both pleasant and unpleasant experiences from your past. It is from these events that you learnt what it means to be human while at the same time remaining, in essence, divine. If there is a particularly painful experience, use your will to shatter the glass into a thousand pieces and affirm that the past has no hold on you. It is a mere reflection of what has been. The only reality is now.

Hands and arms

With the use of our hands and arms, we put into action our capacity for giving and receiving, the exercising of our will and the expression of our creativity. Through touch, we familiarize ourselves with our world and sustain our bodies by feeding ourselves. Debilitating ailments in these limbs and joints, such as rheumatoid arthritis, could be the outward manifestation of emotional rigidity, the belief that we cannot alter the world and a desire to be out of touch with reality.

Visualization: Imagine that your hands and arms are caked in a grey clay that makes it impossible to move your fingers. Now immerse them in a bowl of steaming liquid that gives off an intoxicating smell. It should be something that reminds you of a happy time in your life such as the scent of flowers in your grandparents' garden, the smell of the sea or freshly baked bread. Sense the warm liquid softening the grey shell until it dissolves into the liquid and permeates the skin, muscles, joints and bones to restore the feeling to your fingers. Now fashion something new out of the sticky clay, something that symbolizes what you are going to achieve in the near future. Then wash your hands in the liquid and dry them until every trace of the clay is gone. Alternatively, visualize soaking your hands in a luminous liquid that saturates and revitalizes every cell.

Head

When there is a conflict between the head and the heart, between the emotions and the intellect, we can manifest that tension in the form of a migraine, often when we know that it will elicit sympathy and attention from the person who is the cause or focal point of that conflict.

Visualization: Imagine a sphere of radiant white light above the crown of your head. Draw it down into the region corresponding to the Brow Chakra, and visualize it illuminating the inside of your head as it dissolves the tension in your forehead and jaw. Before you come out of the meditation, tense the muscles in your face by making a wide grin, and then relax.

Heart

The heart may be the symbol of love in western mythology, but on a purely physical level it is the vital organ that pumps blood around the body. As such, it is more likely to malfunction if one feels constrained in any way, or is under extreme stress, than for any reason to do with love.

Visualization: Take several deep breaths and exhale slowly, forming a silent 'F' sound to expel the very last dregs of stale air from the lungs. As you do so, imagine that you are expelling a dark cloud of dust and debris from your chest. Now replenish your body with the life force, in the form of a warm radiant light with each intake of fresh air until the centre of your chest is aglow with warmth from within.

Kidneys

If an individual is unable to process their emotions – particularly if they feel unable to resolve or influence a difficult relationship – they might express this block by creating kidney stones that disrupt the clearing and filtering process in the body.

Visualization: Soften the Heart Chakra by meditating on compassion or on anger, whichever is relevant. Then imagine this unconditional love in the form of a deep yellow sphere flowing through the arteries and veins to dissolve the stones in the kidney.

Liver

Despondency, regret and bitterness can upset the liver, which is concerned with the critical process of detoxification and maintaining the balance of nutrients in the body.

Visualization: Imagine taking a long, cooling drink of a thick, milk-like tonic, and sense this shot of nutrients and minerals saturating your bones, muscles and skin, just as a sponge soaks up water.

Shoulders

Aches and pains in the neck and shoulders are often a direct result of tension and stress as we attempt to shrug off what we consider to be too much responsibility. However, they can also be a symptom of inflexibility in our attitude to life. It is unreasonable to expect to go through life without having to shoulder our share of responsibilities.

Visualization: Imagine that you have a large sack of grain on your shoulders that you are to carry to the end of a long, winding, dirt road. There is a small hole in the sack, and with each step a thin stream of grain runs out, making your burden lighter. Whenever you stop to rest, you can look back and see the trail of seed that will sprout into strong plants marking your trail. Do not be in a hurry to reach the end of the road. The sack of seed that you carry is not a burden unless you think of it as such.

Skin

Skin ailments are invariably linked to problems associated with self-image, prompting the sufferer to manifest an unconscious desire to 'get out of their skin'. Eczema, for example, can be an unconscious reaction to an irritation that the sufferer finds difficult to express in words.

Visualization: Imagine that you are stepping into a bath of steaming, scented water. Luxuriate in its warmth and healing properties, as the oils coat your skin in a protective layer; this is like a transparent second skin which will dry immediately on contact with the air. When you are ready to emerge from the healing bath, climb out and gently dab yourself dry with thick, soft towels.

Crystal visualization therapy

You do not need to own the crystals described below to benefit from their energy; you can generate the same healing frequencies within yourself using visualization, since the crystals serve only as a visual stimulus for the universal life force within your own body.

some will create a tingling sensation, others heat . . .

. . . and others may stimulate the chakras

Visualizing the crystals

'Crystals reminded the ancients of the multifaceted inner worlds.'

Aldous Huxley

Lie flat on a mat or on your bed, close your eyes and establish a regular rhythm of breathing. When you feel suitably relaxed, envisage the crystals (described opposite) being placed on the appropriate part of the body, one at a time, and become acutely aware of the different qualities of energy emanating from each. Some will create a tingling sensation, others heat; and some may stimulate the chakras until you feel the vortices of energy whirling within you. Once you have experienced the effects of the various crystals you can work on one particular part of the body that you believe needs special attention by simply visualizing the corresponding crystal being applied to that part. Feel free to give yourself the complete treatment, however, whenever you feel the need to revitalize yourself after an illness, or just to tone up and rebalance the chakras.

Crystals for each chakra

Crown Chakra: agates, which come in many colours, for general healing; translucent pink rose-quartz, the stone of compassion and creativity, for calm.

Brow or Third Eye Chakra: amethyst, a purple quartz, for creativity, clear thinking, insomnia, grief and migraines.

Throat Chakra: aquamarine, a pale blue silicate, for sore throats, toothache and nervous disorders.

Heart Chakra: jade, which comes in various colours; translucent green emerald for equilibrium; green peridot for the digestion; yellow or green sapphire for stability.

Solar Plexus Chakra: citrine, a warm yellow stone with a hint of orange, for emotional ailments.

Sacral Chakra: ruby, a red corundum crystal, or garnet, a deep purple-red gemstone containing iron, for vital energy, improving circulation, the alleviation of fatigue and depression, and bladder problems.

Root Chakra: black onyx for leg, foot and lower back trouble.

In addition, you could visualize clutching green aventurine, which is effective in relieving the symptoms of skin complaints; a red or orange carnelian for rheumatism; red jasper for liver and kidney ailments; blue lapis lazuli for heart complaints; green malachite for asthma; and opal, which comes in a variety of colours, for breathing problems and bronchial infections.

Colour therapy

The use of colours in meditation is one of the most effective methods of impressing an idea on the unconscious mind, and of provoking an immediate and profound response on an emotional level. Everyone can benefit from using colours in their meditation, as they induce an automatic response from the chakras, the subtle etheric energy centres at key points in the body. After familiarizing yourself with the various colours and their corresponding chakras, you could choose to concentrate on one area in particular to assist with a specific problem, or you might simply enter a meditative state and 'ask' for whichever colour you need at that moment in your life. The colour will then appear in your mind's eye, either in abstract form or in the form of an object associated with that shade.

Colour meditation

Begin by focusing on the breath.

Visualize the colour red in any form that appears spontaneously to your mind's eye. You might imagine a red coat, a red carpet, a field of red flowers or even the blood pumping around inside your body. Red is the colour of physical energy and corresponds to the Sacral Chakra beneath the navel. Stimulating this energy centre by absorbing yourself in red can assist circulation, overcome lethargy and even dissolve the crystals that cause arthritis.

Now visualize the colour yellow, which corresponds to the Solar Plexus Chakra – the seat of the emotions – and allow any knots to unravel or blockages to be released. Do not be surprised if you become emotional at this point. Meditating on this chakra can release suppressed feelings that you were unlikely to have been consciously aware of, but which need to be cleared. In addition, it can be effective in eradicating digestive disorders. Its symbolic association with the sun also makes it an ideal colour for revitalizing and regenerating the body after a debilitating illness.

'And life is colour
and warmth
and light
And a striving
evermore for
these.'

Julian Grenfell

Next visualize the colour green, corresponding to the Heart Chakra. Contemplating this colour can help to cultivate compassion, and is therefore very useful in helping to overcome anger and resentment. Green is symbolic of nature, the dimension where the spiritual and physical worlds meet and manifest in harmony. Absorbing this colour in a visualization exercise can bring serenity and the ability to overcome nervous anxiety.

Now visualize the colour blue, which corresponds to the Throat Chakra and determines your ability to communicate. Contemplating this colour will enable you to express your thoughts and feelings more easily. Its inherent soothing quality makes it a prime healing colour, bringing relief from many ailments.

Contemplating the colour violet should stimulate the Third Eye Chakra in the centre of your forehead, the focus of intuition and the imagination. Meditating on this colour will improve memory and concentration, stimulate the flow of ideas and make it easier to visualize what you really want from life. It will also help to open communication with the Higher Self when you require inner guidance.

The final colour is white, corresponding to the Crown Chakra above your head. This is symbolic of the life force and is particularly effective in providing a sense of protection in times of danger and relieving mental problems such as anxiety. Absorb yourself in the Divine light and lose all sense of self.

37

Mind medicine

Many spiritual traditions and New Age groups teach that, as well as being able to heal the body, the mind can create its own reality in another, non-physical dimension. If that is so, whatever we visualize during meditation could become a reality on an inner level – in the unconscious. By programming the unconscious mind with positive symbols, we should be able to use the power of imagination to establish a pattern for healing so that we have only to visualize certain symbols and colours to trigger the required biological response from the body's own defence system.

The medicine room

Make yourself comfortable, close your eyes and establish a regular relaxed rhythm of breathing.

When you are ready, visualize a flight of steps leading down into a basement room with a large, red cross on the door. You try the handle and, finding that the door is not locked, you enter. It is light and airy and lined with shelf upon shelf of bottles and boxes, all neatly labelled and orderly.

The domed ceiling is made of glass, decorated with a five-pointed star in a circle, the symbol of balance and of the elements in equilibrium within each human being. The chequered floor, formed from black and white tiles, is a reminder that the natural state of the universe is equilibrium, the balance of complementary forces: energy and matter, active and passive, male and female, and so on. Know that it is your natural state to be in balance and therefore in good health.

You may find a doctor or nurse waiting in the room to offer a diagnosis and point out where the cure can be found, or you may feel instinctively drawn to a particular box or bottle. Look at the label carefully and remember the colour of the medicine; it will most likely have a symbolic significance. Identifying the ailment in this way is halfway towards effecting a cure. How often have you left the doctor's surgery feeling a lot better simply because you have been told that whatever your problem is, it can be cured?

When you take the medicine in the visualization, go through the motions of opening the bottle, measuring out the dose and so on, and become acutely aware of the sensation of swallowing the solution or pills. The more detail you can bring to the image in your mind, the more vivid will be the impression left on the unconscious.

Some people are anxious at the thought of opening themselves up to 'spirit guides', as they imagine them to be, but it is more likely that the figure will be a projection of your own unconscious or Higher Self. If you feel uncomfortable about receiving help in this way, you simply have to state in your mind that you do not require it, and your wish will be respected. There is nothing to fear – like attracts like.

'To perceive a distant reality as real is the function of imagination.'

Colin Wilson

Pain relief

There is an enormous amount of both scientific and anecdotal evidence to suggest that the mind can assist in the healing process. The discovery that meditation can have profound physiological effects on the body, such as stimulating the secretion of endorphins (the body's natural painkillers), led to the development of 'biofeedback' during the 1970s, in which patients use a form of meditation for pain and stress relief. Yet anyone can prove the effectiveness of meditation as a method of pain relief for themselves, whether they suffer physically, emotionally or in the mind, by working with the following visualizations.

'Whatever you do, don't shut off your pain; accept your pain and remain vulnerable. However desperate you become, accept your pain as it is, because it is in fact trying to hand you a priceless gift: the chance of discovering, through spiritual practice, what lies behind sorrow.'

Sogyal Rinpoche

The blanket

Sit in a comfortable chair and allow yourself to sink into deep relaxation.

When you feel sufficiently relaxed, envisage a thick, full-length blanket being wrapped snugly around you. The colour of it will come spontaneously to mind and may have a symbolic significance which you can look into later. But for now, simply enjoy the relief it brings and the penetrating heat which envelops your skin.

The blanket is comforting and gives you a sense of security. Become aware of its all-enveloping warmth that penetrates your physical body and, deeper still, into the very essence of your being, to the source, not just the symptoms. In time, it numbs all physical sensation, leading to a sense of detachment.

Now begin to visualize the pain as dark matter, as smoke or grit, being drawn out of the core of your being, through the physical body to be absorbed by the blanket, leaving your body cleansed.

When you feel that the last grain of this dark matter has left you, cast aside the soiled blanket and see it disintegrate as it touches the ground. It is gone, and the pain has gone with it.

To revitalize and centre yourself, close the meditation by visualizing a sphere of dazzling bright light over your head. Draw it slowly all the way down to your feet and watch as it dissolves into the floor. Return to waking consciousness.

The cleansing pool

Another effective meditation involves visualizing a pool or basin of clear or coloured water (accept whichever image comes spontaneously to mind). When this image is stable in your mind's eye, simply step into the pool or bathe the affected area of your body, and watch as the pain dissolves in the water like ink.

Channelling the pain

A third method involves visualizing yourself holding a rock, and imagining the pain channelled like lightning through your body into the rock, which cracks and crumbles into a fine powder. You could also visualize yourself in a garden, park or field, where you embrace a tree through which you 'ground' the pain, freeing you from its grip. Always go with whatever image feels right for you at the time. And don't worry about how vividly you can visualize. It is the strength of your will which affects the cure.

Self-hypnosis

Hypnosis has been proven to be highly effective in helping to eradicate fears and phobias, and in alleviating the causes and symptoms of psychosomatic, or stress-related, illnesses. It is possible to adapt the basic technique to form part of a meditation exercise, enabling anyone to treat themselves and enjoy similar benefits. However, care should be taken in creating the affirmations, or positive suggestions, which are to be programmed into the unconscious mind. Keep your chosen sentences short, simple and unambiguous. For example, use 'I have no fear of flying – it is perfectly safe' rather than 'I'm not going to be afraid of flying any more', which is more likely to reinforce the fear than dispel it. The following exercise is a basis for self-hypnosis and, as your ability to sit in silent meditation for longer periods increases, you should feel confident about exploring the landscape of this inner world. You may find it useful to supplement the exercise with a recording of suitably relaxing music or natural sounds, which will act as a useful trigger to bring you back to waking consciousness. When the recording ends, the atmosphere will be dispelled and you will become aware of your surroundings once again.

keep your chosen sentences short, simple and unambiguous . . .

you feel serene and peaceful . . .

Putting yourself under

Begin by focusing on the breath, as always, but with each exhalation say silently to yourself 'R-e-l-a-x', and pause for a moment before taking the next breath.

When you feel sufficiently relaxed and centred, visualize yourself standing at the top of a winding staircase which leads down to an elegant entrance hall. Say to yourself: 'I am going to walk slowly down these stairs, becoming more relaxed and peaceful with each step, and when I reach the bottom I will be in a deep state of relaxation and open to the positive suggestions that I wish to absorb.'

Now begin your descent, one step at a time, saying: 'one, relax ... two, calm ... three, peace ... four, going deeper ... five, down ... six, deeper ... seven, leaving my cares behind ... eight, into peace ... nine, into calm ...ten, be still.'

You find the hall is empty and silent. You feel serene and peaceful here in a world between waking and dreaming. The only illumination comes from a glass panel in the front door which sends a shaft of light on to the floor. Look upon this blank canvas and repeat your chosen affirmation slowly three times.

If you do not have a specific problem to solve, the repetition of any positive affirmation will be beneficial.

When you are ready, you can return to waking consciousness by ascending the stairs and counting down from ten to one as you do so, or you can pass through the door into the garden beyond and enjoy the serenity until you are ready to end the exercise in the usual way. Alternatively, you can use this technique for self-hypnosis before going to sleep, allowing yourself to drift off once you have repeated your affirmations. This technique is particularly helpful if you have trouble sleeping, and may even provide an answer to your problem in symbolic form for you to ponder the next morning.

'The mind . . . in itself can make a heaven of hell, a hell of heaven.'

John Milton

2 Emotions

Mastering your emotions

Getting in touch with our feelings if we have been bottling things up might be therapeutic, but constantly analysing and attuning ourselves to our emotions can only result in becoming self-absorbed. What we need is to observe our emotions with detachment, and accept the fact that we are not responsible for what we feel. We cannot control our feelings, which are constantly changing, but we can control our reactions to them.

raise your awareness of how fluid your emotions can be · · ·

'Music informs us that we are creatures of feeling, that our feelings are valid, that there is nothing wrong about experiencing them'

Joanne Crandall
Self-transformation Through Music

The emotional journal

You can practise this mindfulness meditation at any time, whatever mood you are in. It will raise your awareness of how fluid your emotions can be and also help you to accept that a wide range of emotions is a perfectly normal part of human nature.

When you are suitably relaxed, close your eyes and mentally review your day from the present back to the moment you awoke this morning. Consider what mood you were in an hour ago. How would you describe your feelings? Go back further. Describe the mood you were in two hours ago, this evening, this afternoon, at lunch and so on.

Did your mood change because of what someone else said, or because of the way they acted? Are you impervious to the moods of others? Few of us are that self-possessed. Were your feelings consistent throughout the day? If so, you must be an extremely rare individual.

Now review the previous day in the same way and become aware of how mercurial you have been. Unless you were subject to violent mood swings for no particular reason, why not learn to accept that this mutability is part of what makes us human.

Beating the blues

'Music is God's way of colouring sound.'

John M. Ortiz
The Tao of Music

Before you begin this meditation, look through your music collection and choose three popular songs, or one longer piece of instrumental music, that expresses your current mood, be it sadness, disappointment or depression. Record these on to a cassette, or whatever format you prefer. This segment should not last longer than ten minutes. Then select a batch of songs or an instrumental which is distinctly mid-tempo to match the mood you would like to move into, and add these to the tape. Finally, pick an assortment of songs or an instrumental piece that can be characterized as upbeat, and complete the recording with these.

The process of choosing suitable music is a meditation in itself, and will usually be enough to distract you from negative thoughts and restore your emotional equilibrium. If not, rewind the tape, make yourself comfortable, close your eyes and enter meditation. Immerse yourself in the music. Allow it to conjure up memories from the past or abstract imagery symbolic of the mood that you are in. Accept whatever reaction it produces. You may find yourself becoming upset. If so, let go and let it flow. Take the opportunity to clear these negative feelings that might not have dissolved otherwise.

Keep the tape for the next time your emotions threaten to overwhelm you and you will doubtless find it as effective as the first time. Many people choose classical or new age music for meditation, but ethnic or world music is ideal for freeing the emotions and stirring the soul. Much of it originates from cultures which have a strong traditional link with the earth and with universal spiritual energies.

Overcoming nerves

Nervousness and anxiety are rooted in a lack of self-confidence and the erroneous belief that we are somehow more vulnerable than everyone else. The first step towards overcoming anxiety is to realize and accept that we are not unique. Every human being is subject to fears and anxieties of one kind or another, but the person who overcomes these natural feelings has simply accepted that fact and stopped trying to fight their fear. The thing we fear is rarely as bad as we imagine it to be. What we really fear is having our character tested and found wanting. We all have the potential to overcome whatever difficulties we have attracted in order to test ourselves, but we need to focus on our response to these perceived problems and not on the problem itself. It is only by overcoming, or at least learning to live with, our anxieties that we can grow and evolve. This five-minute meditation can considerably reduce nervousness and improve performance at job interviews, examinations and so on, and it will also prove beneficial as part of a daily relaxation routine.

Exercise: calming and centring

Sit up straight, with your feet flat on the floor, shoulder width apart. Rest your palms on your thighs, or cup them, supporting one another, in your lap.

Begin by focusing on the breath. Take deep, regular breaths, inhaling for a count of four, pausing for a count of two, and then exhaling for a count of four. Hold for a count of two, before repeating the cycle.

Visualize a large ball of intense white light beneath your feet. Feel the warmth of it as you begin to draw it up very slowly through the soles of your feet. Soak it up as a sponge soaks up water. Draw it up your calves to your knees, then on up through your thighs, relaxing the tension in your legs. It is warming your waist, your lower back and your solar plexus, the seat of the emotions, where it dissolves the knots and frees the energy that you will release when you need to project your positive personality.

Absorb the light into your chest, your neck, your upper back and shoulders. It loosens the tension in your throat, freeing your ability to communicate, and illuminates your face. The light fills the crown of your head and dissolves all tension in your forehead, leaving you feeling relaxed and clear-headed.

Bathe in this light for as long as you wish. Know that it is yours to call upon at any time you require and that, once infused with its revitalizing energy, you are calm, centred and supremely confident.

'Danger itself fosters the rescuing power.'

Friedrich Hölderlin

the thing we fear is rarely as bad as we imagine it to be . . .

Getting a grip on fear

fear increases physical pain and exacerbates anxiety · · ·

It may be a cliché, but there is a lot of truth in the saying 'There is nothing to fear but fear itself'. All of us become anxious to one degree or another when we have to go to the dentist, attend a job interview or face living on our own after a separation or bereavement, for example. We would not be human if we did not have these feelings, but it is how we react to such situations that determines the degree to which we intensify the experience. Fear increases physical pain, exacerbates anxiety and elongates the grieving period when we lose someone we love or end a long-term relationship. As the following exercises illustrate, the first stage of overcoming fear is to accept that it is a natural, instinctive response to a potentially stressful situation, but that we must overcome our fears in order to become more balanced, responsible and mature human beings.

'Feel the fear and do it anyway.'

Susan Jeffers

Banishing fear with the breath

The simplest method of dispelling immediate anxiety is also the most effective. Simply take the deepest breath that you can, and hold it for a moment before exhaling. The result is instantaneous. It not only restores the heartbeat to its regular rhythm and reduces the flow of adrenaline but it also allows a pause in which you can reassume control, calm your mind and clarify your thoughts.

Now take that a stage further. Imagine that you are drawing up the anxiety in the form of stale air or smoke from deep within your body with the in-breath, and dispersing it into the ether with the out-breath. This can be done with your eyes open, prior to and even during whatever situation or activity is causing you unnecessary anxiety. You will be surprised how much better you feel.

Bursting the balloon

If you need a visualization to practise before the event itself, close your eyes, relax and take a long, deep breath. When you exhale, imagine that you are blowing up a balloon (let the colour come spontaneously, as it may have a symbolic significance). Then pause before taking another breath. Each time you exhale, imagine that you are filling the balloon with this feeling of anxiety or fear until it is out of your system. When the balloon is stretched to bursting, mentally tie the knot sealing your fear inside. Then take great pleasure in popping the balloon and dispersing these negative feelings into the ether.

The worst-case scenario

We can live only in the present moment, so there is nothing to be gained by dwelling on something that might never happen, or that might not be as bad as we imagine it might be. All this does is create suffering for ourselves in the present. Every moment we indulge our fear for no reason is a moment lost. What is happening right now is the only reality that we can experience.

What we really fear is the unknown. So take the fear out of the unknown by taking control of your response to it. One way you can do this is to prepare the conscious mind for each possible eventuality or outcome by visualizing the scene and the reactions of those involved. Imagine the worst that can happen in the circumstances, and give it over to your Higher Self to find a solution or the strength to see you through if it really does happen. Be rational and practical – there is a solution to every problem, but it is often obscured to your conscious mind by your churning emotions and irrational expectations. Trust that, in quiet contemplation, that still, small voice will come through with the inspiration or idea that you need to resolve the situation.

Phobias and how to cure them

Phobias are irrational fears, but they can have a very real and debilitating effect on our lives. They usually originate in childhood, and often symbolize a repressed anxiety. They can be very difficult to identify, particularly if they are being used by the unconscious to signify a deeper fear. For example, arachnophobia (fear of spiders) is generally accepted by orthodox contemporary psychiatry in some cases to symbolize a fear of the unknown or of a domineering mother. However, once the origin has been identified, it is usually enough to rid the object of its power. Have patience when you are probing this deep into the unconscious. Think of yourself as digging for fragile relics rather than hidden treasure. Practise these exercises periodically and probe gently.

Facing the fear

Visualize yourself facing your fear in easy stages. If, for example, you have a fear of heights, imagine climbing the first flight of stairs in a multistorey building and looking out of the window when you reach the first-floor landing. Then go up one storey at a time until you reach the top, but take your time. You can leave the ascent to the top until a later session if you wish. If you have a fear of spiders, visualize a tiny spider trapped under a glass. Would you run from such a small creature? Of course not. It's not the spider itself that you are frightened of, you have projected your fears on to something which it is socially accepted to fear. Now imagine a slightly larger spider and sense how frightened it must be of you, a giant by comparison. With each subsequent mediation your fear will diminish. Using meditation in this way helps to overcome deep-rooted phobias, as it prepares the mind for the moment when the fear must be confronted.

Probing the unconscious

Take three deep breaths and relax into the meditative state. Now ask yourself 'What is the cause of my irrational fear of X'? slowly three times.

Then fix your inner eye on a point of light in the far distance, and feel yourself drawn towards it. It will open to present a scene, probably from childhood, but possibly from a previous incarnation. Do not try to analyse what you see. Simply accept and observe with detachment whatever images arise.

Ask the question again. Once you have the answer, affirm in your own words that you recognize the source of your irrational fear. Now 'let go' of the memory by withdrawing from the scene and watching as it disappears into the distance.

Past life regression

For people who believe in reincarnation, such as Buddhists, it is possible that some phobias might represent 'unfinished business' carried over from a previous life. Use this variation on the previous exercises to probe the unconscious for relevant memories and then clear the fear.

Take three deep breaths and relax. Ask yourself 'Does the cause of my irrational fear originate in a past life?' Fix your eye on a pinpoint of light in the distance and follow it. When you emerge on the other side, look down at your clothes and footwear. What can you tell about yourself and the period?

> 'Nothing can exist in our reality unless we feed it energy. By empowering our fears we cause a tremendous drain of our energy.'
>
> Betty Bethards
> *Seven Steps to Developing your Intuitive Powers*

Take your time to explore your surroundings. When you are ready, repeat the question and open yourself to the answer. Do not be afraid; these are only images from the unconscious. If you feel uncomfortable, come out of the meditation by counting slowly down from ten to one and opening your eyes. You can try again another day.

If you receive an answer, you will instinctively know what to do next. If you need to ask forgiveness for a past action, do so (or practise the visualization on page 78), but do not dwell on it. Clear what you have seen from your mind and move on. If it is an emotional or physical issue, give yourself healing (see page 18) in any form that feels appropriate. Remember, however, that the ego and unconscious can play tricks. Do not take anything that is revealed to you at face value. If in doubt, ask your Higher Self for guidance.

Anger

Anger arises from our inability to control events that threaten to disrupt the orderly nature of our world. The first step towards coping with anger is therefore to accept that we cannot impose our will upon the universe or upon other people. The only thing we can control is ourselves. It is not being pessimistic to expect problems, but realistic. On a practical level, the best we can do is to engage in a form of damage limitation by anticipating what might happen and taking appropriate action to prevent it, or at least contain it; just as a sensible parent, to limit danger, will remove all sharp objects from within their child's reach and ensure that no toys can get under their own feet.

Channelling the energy

No matter how centred, detached or grounded we might be, we all feel anger at one time or another. When we do, we need to channel this energy in a harmless way; otherwise we risk poisoning our system. The most effective method of controlling anger is to channel the adrenaline into an activity, preferably one that will make you feel better at the end of it. Punching a cushion might be effective, but digging the garden or jogging will direct a negative emotion towards a positive purpose, leaving you with the feeling that you have actually achieved something, and not just control over your emotions. The following exercise alerts the unconscious mind to how dangerous anger can be, and implants an image that will help to channel it out of your system.

A house aflame

Make yourself comfortable, close your eyes and take several deep breaths from the diaphragm. This will clear much of the tension from the solar plexus, the seat of the emotions, and should be sufficient to expel the pressure from your system. Now continue with the visualization.

> 'Anger is a short madness.'
>
> Horace

Imagine you are standing in a beautiful garden. It is a garden that you have created with love over a lifetime, a garden that you return to whenever you need to find peace and remind yourself how beautiful the world can be. By now, your anger should be considerably reduced.

Now become aware of the residue of anger that still remains in your head and in the solar plexus. Visualize this as a red-hot sphere burning you from the inside. Push it down and out of your body through the soles of your feet and into the ground. Watch as it spreads like a flame through the dry grass towards the flowerbeds, threatening the ornamental trees and the features you have laboured so hard and long to create. Then, just as the flames begin to lick at the edges of the flowers, a cloudburst overhead extinguishes the fire and showers you with refreshing rain.

As you once again admire the garden in the warmth of the emerging sunlight, consider how close you came to destroying your own creation and affirm that you will not risk indulging in such negative emotions again.

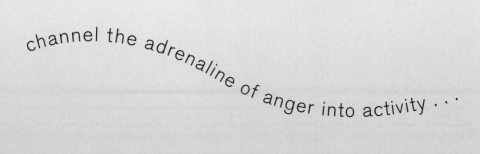

channel the adrenaline of anger into activity . . .

Controlling your temper

Modern society has conditioned us to be obsessive about our weight and our looks, encouraging us to diet and spend hours working out in the gym; but little or no time is spent learning to control the one truly ugly aspect of human nature – anger. If you spend just five minutes a day practising the following visualization, you will feel far better about yourself than you would after an hour's physical exercise and everyone you live and work with will feel better too!

Imagine yourself as you were when you were a child. See yourself playing happily with your brother or sister or best friend. A moment later, you are arguing over a toy. They snatch it from you and you grab it back. There is a scuffle and you start a fight. You pull their hair; they pull yours. You both get red in the face, and in a moment the friendly smiling faces have been distorted by anger and hatred. You hit out and they hit you back. You stumble and fall, breaking the toy

is it worth risking your life to show how angry you can be?

that you could not share and hurting yourself in the process. You both start crying, each trying to show how hurt you are by crying louder than the other. It is all so unfair. Now an adult comes in, someone who loves you and feels for you, but who also finds the melodrama just too silly to be sour with you. They laugh and hug both of you, encouraging you to make up and be friends again.

As adults, we think our anger is justified, but if you visualize the scene just described you will see that invariably our outbursts are as irrational as those of a child. Hug your Inner Child, forgive it and, above all, learn to laugh at yourself as easily as you did when you were a child.

The inner thermometer

The next time you feel your emotional temperature rising, imagine the anger as a boiling red liquid in your solar plexus. Visualize it rising up the centre of your chest towards your throat like the mercury inside a thermometer. As it approaches your head, try to recall those cartoons and comedies you must have seen as a child, in which an angry or sick character gets so irate or ill that his temperature shatters the thermometer.

Now take a long, deep breath and consider if it is really worth the risk of bursting a blood vessel for whatever is causing your blood to boil. A large percentage of strokes are brought on by stress, frustration and anger. Is it worth risking your life to show someone how angry you can be?

Hostility and hatred

Meditation is normally concerned with serenity, peace of mind and positive thoughts, but occasionally it is necessary to shock the ego out of its deceitful and self-defeating mind games in order to restore a healthy balance. If you have seen a lot of grisly horror films, you should not have any trouble conjuring up the imagery in this visualization.

The scarecrow

When you are suitably relaxed, imagine yourself brooding on whatever is causing you to feel hatred and hostility; as you do so, see the light and the life force draining out of your body. As your vitality seeps away, your body withers from fingers to toes, consumed by the hatred and hostility you feel towards the other person. If you do not let go of this darkness in your Heart Centre, you risk becoming a shadow of your former self, a scarecrow animated only by hatred.

Be aware of what you are doing to yourself, and let it go. If you do not, you risk ruining your relationships, your health and becoming thoroughly dislikable, even to those who care for you most.

Visualize a red-hot coal or a black ember in the centre of your chest, and ease it out. Let it fall to the ground and crumble to ash, as you affirm that you disown these negative feelings.

The black hole

In astronomy, a black hole is a dying star 'whose gravity is so great that nothing can escape from it, not even light'. An analogy can be made between this astronomical phenomenon and the self-destructive element in human beings. We are electrobiological organisms, formed from cosmic particles millions of years old. As such, we may be capable of attracting negative energy in much the same way as a black hole in space sucks in debris until it implodes, creating antimatter or a vacuum in space.

Hatred, hostility and other negative emotions invert our mental energy as we turn in on ourselves until the pressure creates headaches and depression – the former is the physical symptom and the latter is the emotional consequence.

If you feel yourself giving in to negative thoughts of any kind, enter meditation and imagine yourself sitting in shadow, attracting dark matter in the form of fine clouds of dust as you become more self-absorbed. As the dust settles on you, the light of the life force is growing weaker. At this critical point, affirm that nothing is worth living in darkness for, and that the spark of life will not be stifled by self-pity or any other life-denying emotion. Visualize the light of the life force intensifying in your Heart Centre, and sense the warmth radiating outwards as the darkness is dispelled and the dust particles dispersed to the four corners of the universe. Bask in the radiance of your aura, and expand your awareness to see with your inner eye the full spectrum of colours that comprise your own life-affirming energy field.

You can easily train yourself to see your aura. Simply place your hand against a plain surface and soften your gaze so that you focus on the background, rather than your hand. After a few minutes you should be able to see an electric blue outline which is the first layer of etheric energy surrounding the body. With practice, you will become more sensitive, then you will be able to diagnose the physical, emotional and mental states of your family and friends from the dominant colours of their aura.

> 'Because the law of karma is inevitable and infallible, whenever we harm others, we are directly harming ourselves ...'
>
> Sogyal Rinpoche

Improving relationships

As the Indian guru Krishnamurti once remarked, we can only truly know ourselves in the give and take of a relationship, not in abstraction or isolation. It is also true that we can only grow and mature through the peaceful, reasoned resolution of a conflict, not by walking away from difficulties, nor by imposing our will upon another person.

unburden yourself of what has been eating away inside you . . .

Resolving conflict

Use this variation on the empty chair visualization (see page 78) whenever you feel the need to get to the truth of a difficult situation.

Imagine you are seated opposite the person with whom you are having difficulties. See them as being as confused and hurt as you are. Now say whatever is on your mind. Unburden yourself of all that has been eating away inside you, and feel the pressure of this burden being lifted from your chest.

Now shift your perception to the other chair, and look back at yourself through the other person's eyes. How do they perceive you? What do they see and hear? Were you perhaps being too assertive or too certain that you were in the right?

> 'When you affirm your rightness in the universe, then you cooperate with others easily and automatically as part of your own nature, You, being yourself, help others be themselves.'
>
> Jane Roberts

Assume their mannerisms and their attitude as you answer yourself in their voice. What does this reveal that you were previously unaware of?

You can end the meditation either by returning in your mind to your own chair and closing down or, if you feel it is appropriate, by going straight into the following visualization.

The hug

This meditation can be practised on its own at any time that you feel the need to reaffirm your love for someone, or to shrug off the residue of any ill feeling existing between you.

Visualize the other person surrounded by an aura of white light. See them doing something that makes you smile, or better still something that makes you laugh.

Recall something they have said to you that made you feel loved and needed.

Now draw them to you and embrace them while affirming the following: 'X and I enjoy a fulfilling and loving relationship. All is well between us. All perceived difficulties have been dissolved.'

Ask them for whatever you need to make you feel better about the relationship. It could be patience, commitment or a declaration of their love. In return, ask what they would like to have from you. You may find that you are surprised at the answer. What your conscious mind or ego demands may not be the same as what is required by the Higher Self in order to make a more lasting and fulfilling relationship.

Heart to heart

Picture the other person sitting opposite you, surrounded by an aura. The dominant colour of this aura corresponds to the mood that you imagine the person to be in. If, for example, they are angry, the colour will be red; if they are confused and upset, you will visualize a muddy mix of yellow, red, orange and brown.

Now soften your Heart Centre by meditating on compassion or forgiveness (see page 78).

Then take the sphere of green, radiant light corresponding to the Heart Chakra from the centre of your chest and cradle it in both hands as if it were a precious glass bowl. Look into it and imagine that you can see within it a spiritual being such as an angel, your inner guide or a compassionate and wise figure from the past. Ask them to bring peace to yourself and the other person by resolving the apparent conflict between you. Then hand the glowing sphere to the other person who takes it to their heart, and watch as it is absorbed into their body. Gradually, the dominant colour in their aura dissolves and they are bathed in a deep, serene blue. This colour corresponds to the Throat Chakra which governs communication.

Affirm in words of your own choosing that you have a constructive and peaceful relationship with all your fellow beings, and that you wish them health and happiness in this life. Finally, thank your guide or angel for their help. When you are ready, return to waking consciousness.

'The most effective way to achieve right relations with any living thing is to look for the best in it, and then help that best into the fullest expression.'

J. Allen Boone

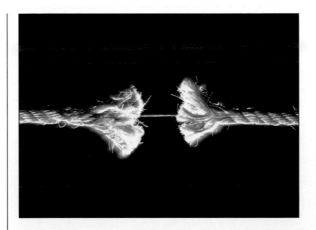

Cutting the ties

If your relationship with a partner or friend is obviously at an end, but one or both of you are finding it difficult to let go, use this visualization to sever the emotional ties.

Imagine you are joined to the other person by long, coloured strands through which your vital energy is flowing. As long as you are in conflict, or unable to break away, you are draining each other of the universal life force and disturbing the natural balance of mind, body and spirit.

Now visualize yourself wielding a sword of light, and cut through each strand with a confident thrust. If you do not like the image, simply pluck out the strands with your fingers, as if they were the tendrils of a clinging vine, and watch as they dry and shrivel on the ground. Feel the sucker being snapped out of the corresponding energy centre, and hear the satisfying 'pop' as you pull it out. The more physical and 'real' you make the experience, the more effective it will be on the inner level.

Finally, visualize a sphere of white light being absorbed through the crown of your head and that of the other person. It revitalizes and restores a state of equilibrium which will remain with you for the rest of the day.

Coping with grief

There is no cure for grief. It is a process that we all have to pass through. The pain of losing someone we love is an inescapable part of the human experience. If we could, by some miracle, be impervious to the pain of separation, we would also be insensitive to love, beauty and happiness – all the positive sensations that make life worth living. However, it is how we respond to loss that determines how much we suffer and to what intensity we feel that loss.

Five stages of grief

The grieving process is not the same for everyone, of course, but there are five identifiable stages that we all have to work through before we can emerge from such a trial, strengthened by the experience. The five stages are disbelief, denial, anger, helplessness and pining. We do not all experience them in that order, or in any discernible order for that matter, as our emotions are in a constant state of flux, but being able to identify what we are going through, and knowing that it is not unique, can be of some comfort. The following visualization will help you to begin to accept your loss and to dissolve the emotional ties that make it such an emotionally draining experience.

Letting go

Make yourself comfortable, close your eyes and focus on your breathing. Breathe from the diaphragm (see page 10) to reduce the strain on your chest muscles and to create a feeling of calm.

When you are suitably relaxed, visualize a dense, white cloud before you, out of which steps the person you loved. See them as they were when they were at their happiest and in perfect health. There is a radiance around them, which is the life force that can never die. Know that their essence is eternal and lives on in the dimension of light, where they will wait until it is your time to cast off the physical form.

'Mourning never ends. It's just as time goes on it erupts less frequently.'

John Bowlby

Embrace them, and tell them how much you loved them. Say whatever comes to mind, and as you do so feel a great weight being lifted from your heart.

Now is the time to say goodbye. See them enfolded by the cloud, which becomes smaller and smaller until it dissolves into a pinpoint of light. Now close down your own energy field and return to waking consciousness.

Although it is best to perform this meditation only once, so that you can say goodbye and let your loved one go, you may feel the need to do it several times in the immediate period after their death.

The book of memories

Another helpful technique is to enter a meditative state and visualize yourself making a scrapbook celebrating the life of the deceased. It is important that you recall both the good and bad aspects of their personality and the difficult times you shared as well as the happy times, so as not to idealize that person. Use mental images to capture key moments in their life as if they were photographs, collect significant objects from the past to put into the book and, finally, write a letter to them describing how you feel and resolving any unfinished business.

3 Mind matters

Stilling the restless mind

Some of the most effective methods of stilling the restless mind are also the simplest. The following exercise is based on one of the fundamental disciplines of meditation – breath control – and can be used to quieten the mind and produce a feeling of profound peace.

The floating feather

Sit up straight with your feet flat on the floor, parallel, shoulder width apart.

Take a long, full breath to fill your lungs. Then exhale as slowly as you can, making a soft 'F' sound to sustain the out-breath for as long as possible. Expel the very last particle of stale air by pushing it out from the diaphragm; then pause before taking the next breath.

Now establish a steady, regular rhythm, pausing between breaths for a count of two and inhaling and exhaling for a count of four. Focus on the air that you are drawing in and sense it circulating around the upper half of your body.

Then, with each exhalation, visualize the air being pushed down into the lower half of your body.

Once you can maintain this rhythm without having to count four-two-four-two, begin the visualization.

Imagine a small, white feather on the ground before you. Watch as it rises a few centimetres off the ground with every intake of breath, and falls again with every exhalation. Visualize it floating in mid-air and lying absolutely still on the ground as you take the pause between breaths. At first, it may be difficult to sustain the image without being distracted by your thoughts or by other images, but with practice you should be able to keep this picture in your mind for five minutes or more.

If, however, you want to develop your ability to visualize vividly and in greater detail take the exercise a stage further by imagining the feather floating and turning in the air as you breathe in and out. The longer you can keep the feather in the air in this way the easier it will be to train the mind to move into more advanced techniques such as creative visualization and pathworking (see pages 96 and 112).

'Yoga is the settling of mind into silence. When the mind is settled, we are established in our essential nature which is unbounded consciousness.'

Patanjali

Calm waters

It is said that during meditation the mind should be as tranquil as the calm waters of a lake. Use this image to quieten the mind during meditation and, if thoughts arise, observe them with detachment as if they were birds crossing the skyline. Then draw your attention gently back to the surface of the water.

When you have used this image a few times, you can vary it by visualizing a single leaf floating gently down to the surface where it sends tiny ripples spreading out towards the shore.

Resist the temptation to elaborate further, as in meditation the rule is the simpler the better. However, if you find images arising spontaneously and in greater detail you may wish to move on to the pathworking exercises (see page 112) where such imagery can have a symbolic significance on a spiritual level. When you feel ready, it could be very revealing to explore beneath the surface of the water which is symbolic of the unconscious.

Serenity and stress relief

A certain amount of stress is necessary to galvanize us into action and help us to achieve our aims, but it can become addictive, which can be extremely debilitating. The focus of your irritation and anxiety may be a symptom of the way you perceive the world and those with whom you find yourself in conflict. As the traditional Buddhist teaching says, 'if you want to change the world, you first have to change yourself'. The first exercise is designed to alleviate the symptoms and cultivate a sense of detachment, while the second works with symbolism to identify the cause.

The cloud

This visualization should be performed lying down on a bed or mat with the head supported by a pillow or cushion. Lie with your arms by your sides but not touching your body, and your legs slightly apart.

Begin by focusing on the breath. Then, when you feel sufficiently relaxed, scan your body from your toes to your head. Tense each muscle in turn, holding it for a few moments before releasing.

Start to take slightly deeper breaths, pausing at the top of the breath and exhaling in two gradual breaths of equal length. Feel your body becoming lighter as you begin to build a cushion of etheric energy under your body. Continue this rhythm and method of breath control or return to the standard two-four-two-four count, with the out-breath performed in a single movement. As always, do whatever feels comfortable and effortless for you.

As you build this cushion of energy under your body, visualize yourself supported by a cloud. As the cloud takes form in your mind's eye, feel it rising gently, carrying you up into the sky. Leave your thoughts and your earth-bound mind behind, and let go.

Now expand your awareness to take in the view below. Visualize a patchwork of fields and the sea beyond, to which you find yourself drifting. Enjoy the floating sensation. Indulge yourself for as long as you like and explore the skies. Absorb the sunlight, the freshness of the air and the silence.

When you are ready, begin to drift back again, returning gradually to earth, to your home, your room and finally to the bed or mat. Feel the weight of your body being supported and ask yourself to identify the source of the stress in your life, and then ask what you can do to alleviate or resolve this. Consider the matter for a few moments before you return to waking consciousness.

'To be at peace in any endeavour, we must release our need to control the outcome.'

Diane Dreher
The Tao of Inner Peace

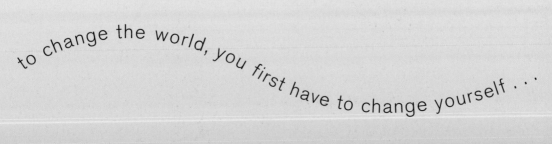

to change the world, you first have to change yourself . . .

The hot-air balloon

A variation on the cloud exercise involves visualizing a hot-air balloon anchored to the ground, weighed down by sandbags. You climb into the basket and release the holding ropes. As you rise slowly into the sky, imagine cutting the sandbags, becoming aware of what they contain as you do so. They symbolize the burdens that are weighing you down. You may not have a clear idea of what they symbolize at first, but in subsequent visualizations they should reveal the source of your stress, which might not be what you originally thought it was.

Releasing the sandbags during a meditation is the first step to identifying the source of stress and accepting the need to be free of them in reality.

The bubble

Another simple method of avoiding stress is to cultivate detachment – a sense of being 'in the world but not of it', to borrow a Buddhist expression.

One of the most effective ways of doing this is to visualize yourself in a thick-skinned bubble, from which you can observe the world going about its business while you remain serene and centred, even in the midst of chaos. In so doing, you will strengthen the aura of energy around yourself, which will lessen the effects of any negative energy emanating from other people. Do not worry that you might be retreating from the world; you are not. You are creating a sacred space in which to take a breath and conserve your vital energy.

Practise this every time you feel that your peace of mind is being threatened by others, and you will find not only that you create a 'thicker skin' to help you survive in the real world, but also that you emanate a quiet strength which will gradually influence your environment for the benefit of all.

Taking time out

Take a few moments out from a potentially stressful situation and walk through this visualization in your mind. The simple act of sustaining the image for a minute or two will be sufficient to moderate your reaction and, in turn, take the heat out of the situation.

Take three deep breaths, holding each for a moment before exhaling very slowly. Now close your eyes and visualize the route you would take to leave the room you are in. Walk through every step in your mind until you are out of the building; then turn right and walk clockwise around the outside of the building before returning the way you came.

If you have the time, take a longer stroll around the neighbourhood. Do not be surprised if a solution to the problem or an appropriate response to the person creating the difficulty occurs to you during your break. Even if you cannot do more than one lap of the building, take time out to give yourself that break, and you will find that it is enough to diffuse the situation.

Worry

If you have a tendency to worry, do not waste vital mental energy on it during the day and risk becoming distracted from what needs to be done. Instead, make a mental note of whatever is worrying you, and visualize putting it in a compartment at the back of your mind for consideration during your next meditation session. When you are relaxed and have the guidance of your Higher Self to call upon, open your 'worry' file and give each item your full attention. This way you will train yourself to break the bad habit of needless fretting. In putting your anxieties into their proper perspective, you will give yourself the necessary space and silence to find a solution to whatever is worrying you.

Alternatively, visualize yourself writing down whatever is worrying you, then attach the sheet of paper to the tail of a kite. Feel the kite tugging to be free as it catches the wind and when the moment feels right release it with your blessing. Watch it sail into a cloudless sky and affirm that the solution will be forthcoming.

Increasing self-awareness

Most of us have neither the time nor the inclination to go to a counsellor or a therapist, but all of us could benefit enormously from regular self-analysis, even if we do not have a major issue to resolve. If you can be rigorously honest with yourself, you can use meditation to begin the process of transformation from being self-centred to becoming acutely self-aware. Trusting in your own common sense and intuition in this way is one of the most significant steps in developing an open channel to the unconscious. Before you begin each session of self-analysis, it is advisable – and often revealing – to define your present mood in a word or two. This practice will help you focus on your feelings more easily and increase your self-awareness.

Session 1: personality profiling

Enter into a meditative state and then ask yourself the following questions. Allow sufficient space after each question for the answer to arise from the unconscious.

Which three adjectives would you use to describe the positive aspects of your personality? How do these aspects manifest themselves and what can you do to enhance them?

Which three adjectives would you use to describe the less appealing aspects of your personality? Do you dislike these traits in other people and, if so, how do you react when you identify these traits in others? What might these traits be concealing?

Before ending the session, recall three people from your past whom you admire and three whom you considered to be deliberately obstructive. What did you learn from those you admired, and what did you learn from those you disliked? From whom did you learn more?

Session 2: house of the psyche

A traditional and effective method of self-analysis is to visualize yourself entering a house that is symbolic of your current state of mind. You can explore the various rooms at your leisure, making mental notes of the furniture, fittings, décor and state of repair for later analysis. In *How to Meditate* (Hamlyn, 2000), I have described a typical visit in detail and given possible explanations for the symbolic imagery; but, if you wish to develop your intuitive powers and establish a strong connection with the unconscious, you will need to trust your own ability to translate what you see in the meditation.

use meditation to begin the process of transformation . . .

. . . from being self-centred to becoming acutely self-aware

Session 3: understanding difficulties

'Know thyself.'

Inscription above the ancient Greek temple at Delphi

Whenever you are confronted by a difficult situation, see it as an obstacle that is asking to be overcome. Enter a meditative state and ask yourself the following questions.

How do you react to problems? Do you rise to the challenge or blame others? Do problems often appear insurmountable because you try to enforce a favourable outcome? Do the problems recur because you deny that there is a problem at all? Is it possible that you unconsciously set up that situation in order to learn something from it and, if so, have you ever done this before? Once you are aware of your tendency to do so, the situation is unlikely to occur again.

Seeing yourself anew

We cannot expect to improve our health, enjoy a better quality of life, nurture fulfilling relationships and increase our prosperity if we harbour an unconscious belief that we are not worthy of the best that life has to offer. If we do not love or at least accept ourselves as we are, with our imperfections as well as our qualities, then we are imposing limitations. If there is something that you do not like about yourself, then meditation and affirmations will awaken the willpower you need to make changes or to alter your perspective. You can then begin to clear the conditioning that has created this false imperfect image.

Three faces

Make yourself comfortable, close your eyes and focus on the breath until you have established a steady and regular rhythm.

Now imagine that you are alone in your room in front of a full-length mirror. How do you see yourself? Study your physical characteristics and consider what you like about yourself and what you could do to enhance these features. Now consider what you do not like about yourself, if anything, and consider what you might be able to change. If it is something that cannot be altered, can you learn to accept it as one of the things that makes you unique? Could it be something that you have been conditioned to see as imperfect by others?

What qualities are you particularly proud of? What talents do you possess? How can you develop these further and to what use can you put them?

Which abilities would you like to possess and how can you acquire them?

Now imagine yourself enjoying the company of your friends and family. It might help to recall a specific event, such as a birthday party, when you were laughing together and feeling particularly happy.

Visualize yourself as your friends and family see you. What qualities do they see in you? Do not be surprised if you discover that what they perceive as your best qualities are not the same as those you have identified yourself. The physical characteristics that you consider, or have been conditioned to consider, imperfect may well be completely irrelevant to those who love you.

Finally, return to face the full-length mirror, and see yourself as you would like to be in the future. Imagine that you have achieved all your ambitions, fulfilled your potential in every aspect of your life and are enjoying the rewards of your efforts and success. How have you changed? Again, do not be surprised if the qualities that are now manifest in the mirror are different to those that you believe you possess now.

'The spirit is the true self.'

Cicero

Affirmations

By planting positive suggestions in the unconscious, we can clear any negative conditioning that might be preventing us from reaching our full potential. If the three faces exercise above has revealed issues that you want to work on, simply choose one of the following sentences and repeat it during your daily meditation.

- I am complete and perfect.
- I accept myself as I am.
- I love myself unconditionally and am loved unconditionally by my maker.
- I deserve the very best in life.
- I am empowered by the infinite power of the universe.

After a week, return to the three faces visualization, and note any significant changes so that you can analyse them upon waking.

Forgiveness

One's best and most constant friend is, of course, oneself – or it ought to be. It is as important to forgive ourselves for what we perceive to be our mistakes and failings as it is to forgive others. Yet, if we are unable to untie these emotional knots, we eat ourselves up with resentment until we manifest this dis-ease as physical symptoms. The following exercises are adapted from a form of Gestalt therapy in which patients are encouraged to act out unresolved issues. They have the potential to awaken repressed emotions, so care should be taken.

The empty chair

When you have made yourself comfortable, close your eyes and imagine you are seated opposite the person from whom you wish to elicit forgiveness, or to whom you want to offer forgiveness.

Now say everything that you feel the need to express, until you have cleared what has been gnawing at you.

Then take a few deep breaths and imagine that you are sitting in the other chair looking back at yourself. Take the other person's point of view and respond as you imagine they would to what you have said.

Now make your peace with that person, wish them well in life and watch as they disappear into a ball of radiant white light which gradually fades, leaving an empty chair.

The spiritual counsellor

'We read that we ought to forgive our enemies; but we do not read that we ought to forgive our friends.'

Cosimo de Medici

If you find the previous exercise difficult, you can elicit the figurative help of a spiritual guide, religious figure, family member or even a friend to act as an arbitrator or confessor. Envisage them seated between you and the other party, listening dispassionately to both sides of the argument.

Listen carefully, in case they convey a message to you from the other person. Let them feel your anger, resentment or regret, and sense their ability to release you from this pain.

When you feel it is right to finish, ask for their blessing on both of you and accept it gracefully, because it frees you from a prison of your own making.

Footprints in the sand

A particularly effective way of asking for forgiveness, or eliciting forgiveness for yourself, is to consider the hypothesis that we are all loved unconditionally by whatever we consider to be the creative source in the universe. Commit the essence of the following story to memory, and recall it during your next meditation in order to experience how effectively it can arouse compassion and forgiveness, even in the most troubled heart.

A man who could not bring himself to forgive his own failings and those of his neighbours was visited in a dream by an angel. The angel showed him the events of his life in a series of recorded scenes. The man noticed that for most of his life there had been two sets of footprints, but only one when he had faced his worst crises. He demanded to know why the angel had deserted him when he needed him most, and was told: 'Beloved child, I love you and would never leave you. At those times when you were burdened by sorrow, worry and fear, it was then that I carried you.'

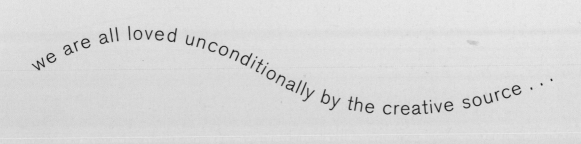

we are all loved unconditionally by the creative source . . .

Accepting change and overcoming difficulties

Many of our problems arise from a fear of change, which is one reason why certain people frequently find themselves in self-destructive relationships with the same type of partner, and others put up with an unsatisfying job year after year. We are creatures of habit. We seek security in the familiar and doubt our capacity to adapt. Yet it is only through new experiences that we can learn who we are and what we are capable of. We all have an instinctive resistance to new environments, new relationships, new demands on our time and talents – in fact anything that appears to challenge our routine. The course of human evolution, however, is a perfect illustration of how we have repeatedly overcome our resistance to change in order to satisfy our curiosity about ourselves and the universe we live in. The following visualization will gradually reduce your resistance to change and implant the idea that the unknown is to be embraced not feared.

'I have learned more from my mistakes than from my successes.'

Sir Humphry Davy

The cave

Imagine you are living in a cave at the dawn of history, huddled around the dying embers of a fire with other members of your tribe. The last scraps of food have been eaten and the waterhole is dry. The dawn is breaking, but the others fear to venture outside. They believe that the shadows on the walls at the entrance to the cave might be those of wild animals. One covers his eyes so as not to see the shadows, another covers his ears so as not to hear them; but you have not heard any animal sounds. It could be the wind making those noises and the trees creating the shadows.

The light of dawn is now breaking through a fissure in the rock far above your head. You decide to leave the stifling air of the cave behind you and make the perilous climb up to the ledge in the roof. You inch your way up, never looking back, but only up towards the warm sunlight which invites you to explore the world outside the cave. With each foothold your anxiety is lessened.

Eventually, you reach the opening and feel the sunlight on your face. You breathe the fresh air and emerge in a lush, tropical paradise with fresh running mountain water and ripe fruit in abundance. There are other people here and they welcome you, offering fresh clothes, food and friendship.

only through new experiences can we learn who we are · · ·

81

Dispelling depression

Depression is a state of mind. It may be triggered by events that can create the false impression that we are not in control of our lives; or in some cases it may be caused by a chemical imbalance in the brain. It is essentially an emotional response, however, and clinical depression has no basis in reality. Through meditation we create our own reality, restoring serenity and stability in the midst of life's uncertainties. The following ten-minute visualization will help to dispel depression and put life into a more positive perspective (see also 'Beating the blues' on page 47).

Begin by closing your eyes and focusing on your breath.

Now visualize yourself in a cavern far beneath the surface of the earth, surrounded on all sides by rock. The stifling, claustrophobic atmosphere is created by your state of mind, but it will lift when you begin your ascent to the surface.

As you become accustomed to your surroundings, details appear out of the darkness. The only light comes from a large pool of clear water at your feet. You kneel down to look into it and see that it is reflecting the light of countless stars, which is breaking through a small fissure directly above you.

Look into the calm, dark, fathomless water and reflect on whatever has led you into the depths. Scoop a palmful of sparkling water from this pure mountain pool

'Humankind learns much faster through adversity. If everything is easy and no obstacle is in our way we never learn anything.'

Dr Elisabeth Kübler-Ross
On Death and Dying

and refresh your face. Wash away the grime. Now drink and wash the dust from your mouth and throat. You are refreshed and ready to return to the surface. Before you do so, however, you remove the heavy backpack that you brought with you and feel how good it is to be finally free of that burden. Look through the contents and examine what you have been carrying. You can leave them here. You no longer need them. They serve no useful purpose.

You look around for a way out, and as you do so the light in the pool grows stronger. The moon emerges from behind a cloud and its reflected light fills the chamber, illuminating a stairway of stone steps that have been carved into the rock.

Begin the long, slow climb back to the surface, all the time looking up into the calming night sky. Visualize yourself emerging from the mountain, to rest stretched out in the soft grass with the sound of the night birds and a gentle breeze in the trees to lull you to sleep.

Allow yourself to sink into a restful sleep, or gradually return to waking consciousness by counting down from five to one. Open your eyes and sit still for a few moments, enjoying the peace you have brought with you.

Exercising your willpower

Most of us believe that we could achieve much more in life if we only had the will to turn our aspirations into action. The fact is that we already possess a certain degree of willpower, otherwise we could not even climb out of bed each morning and get through the day. We exercise our will with every action that we perform, whether we do it reluctantly or not. However, to make the extra effort needed to do something that we do not have to do, we need to persuade our ego, or Inner Child, that it is in our best interests to do so. As with a child, we will get further if we reward good behaviour rather than threaten sanctions if the child does not do what it is told. Therefore, in the following meditations, the element of reward is as important as the aim.

Taking the prize

If we want something very much, we can strengthen our willpower with desire, and together these will drive us towards our goal. So settle on something that you would really love to have when you have attained your goal, something that is in proportion to the achievement. A holiday or a new TV, for example, might

prove a suitable stimulus if you are working towards a qualification, while an evening off relaxing in front of a movie with a takeaway might be enough to prompt you to weed the garden. Whatever treat you choose, envisage it in detail as you meditate, so that it becomes as welcome as an oasis in the desert for the weary traveller.

Exercising your willpower is like exercising any other part of your body. You would not think of starting a new fitness regime with a marathon run, so you should not test your willpower by aiming too high. The following visualization will help strengthen your will by building upon small successes.

One step at a time

The key to strengthening the will is to have a purpose towards which you can channel it, so set yourself a practical goal. This should be something that can be achieved in one day, such as tidying your room or repairing something small that has been annoying you.

When you are sufficiently relaxed, visualize yourself working through the project. Take each stage in detail, noting any possible difficulties that might arise, and consider the solutions. This latter aspect is crucial, because even the most motivated person can falter if they have underestimated the difficulties.

Recall a time in the past when you applied yourself to something when you did not feel motivated, but accomplished it anyway. Take strength from this.

Now visualize yourself completing the task and receiving your reward. When you return to waking consciousness, take the first practical steps to achieving your goal, no matter how small, and then another so that you are committed to seeing it through. If it is worth doing, do not give your ego the chance to persuade you to postpone it.

When you have finally accomplished your chosen task, relish the sense of achievement; but do not neglect to give yourself that reward. Enjoy it – you have earned it.

'The will is like a muscle; it grows stronger with use.'

Dan Millman
Everyday Enlightenment

Addiction and over-indulgence

An addiction is commonly defined as an abnormal dependence on anything that can either stimulate or sedate the senses by altering the chemical balance in the body. The root cause, however, of an insatiable appetite for drugs, alcohol, tobacco, food or even fast cars is likely to be psychological rather than biological. The physical compulsion is often merely a symptom of a psychological malaise: a loss of confidence in oneself, a false perception of the world and an unfounded fear of the future. Addiction is really an expression of our willingness to empower an inanimate object with the ability to enrich our lives. Note, however, that these visualizations are intended to supplement professional medical treatment for the more serious forms of addiction, and not replace it.

'It is not because things are difficult that we do not dare; it is because we do not dare that they are difficult.'

Seneca

Embrace the younger you

The following visualization is designed to undermine the self-destructive impulse that props up this false image and to encourage you to exercise the free will to overcome it.

Make yourself comfortable, relax and then focus on the breath.

When you are ready, visualize yourself as you were when you were at your happiest. No matter how difficult life has been, everyone can recall at least one period in their life when they felt happy, secure, optimistic and, most of all, loved.

Visualize the scene in as much detail as you can. Then focus in turn on the other people who were there, and become aware of their feelings towards you. Know and affirm that they loved you, regardless of how you looked or thought. If you were alone, recall how you felt and what made you feel like that. Know that this capacity to be optimistic and self-contained remains an integral part of your personality.

Know and affirm that you are the very same person that you were then and just as deserving of happiness, love and self-respect. The passing years have not diminished the qualities for which you were and are still loved.

Call out to that younger you and embrace them. Ask them to remain with you as you summon up the strength and will to overcome the self-destructive impulse that currently ensnares you.

Thank them and return to waking consciousness, but retain those images in your mind as long as you can. The more often you practise the meditation, the easier it will be to retain the image through the day and the stronger will be the memory and presence of this contented Inner Child.

Step by step

When you are relaxed, visualize the object of your addiction before you. Now push it away. You do not need it. You rightly resent its power over you, and now affirm your determination to be free from its influence. You may imagine that you are still attached to it by elasticated strings. If so, visualize yourself cutting the strings – the emotional ties that bind you to the object.

Now see yourself walking to the door. As you do so, look back and know that you do not need it as strongly as you did before. Go to the front door, leave the house and walk round the block. Feel how good it is to be free at last, and imagine how good it will be to feel this way all the time. When you return, the object is still there, but it is already losing its appeal.

Try taking a longer walk around the neighbourhood each time you practise the meditation, and close by dropping the object in the dustbin. Each time you practise this visualization, your determination to be free of it will intensify and the object will prove less appealing.

Acquiring self-discipline and practising patience

According to the old saying, 'patience is a virtue', but that is not entirely true. We are not born with patience, nor are we born with its complementary quality, self-discipline. These are attributes that have to be acquired, and if we are not willing to develop them we will learn their value the hard way, by experience.

The child's story

Imagine you are seated in a comfortable chair while a child of three or four plays quietly at your feet. It might be your own child or one that is visiting you. After a few moments, the child looks up and is evidently bursting to tell you something that they consider very important. They are having difficulty finding the right words, but you can see that they want to tell you in their own way and do not want you to interrupt. You must be patient.

The child begins a long story, told in a convoluted way, but if you interrupt they will lose the thread, and also lose confidence at a crucial stage in the story's development. You must keep silent and remain intently interested.

The story itself is not as important as what the child is trying to tell you about how they feel – about you, their family, their fears or their dreams, perhaps. Look into their eyes and sense the effort they are making to communicate and the enthusiasm they have for life. Take a deep breath and hear the story to the end. The expression of glee and satisfaction on the child's face tells its own story, and they hug you for being there when they needed you.

Now, whenever you find yourself in a mundane situation, maybe at work or in a shop, relate to each person you meet in the same way you did to the child. Hear them out with patience and give them your full attention. Even those who appear unfriendly at first might have had that same enthusiasm for life when they were small, but no one listened, and now they too have little time for anyone else.

The model village

Imagine you have been asked to create a model village for a group of disadvantaged children, who are depending on you and believe in you. It does not matter if you have never made anything like this before, or even if you have no craft skills. In this dimension of imagination, you possess all the skills required, and the materials are at hand.

The project will take several separate meditation exercises to complete, over a period of a week or more. There is no rush to complete it, as time does not exist on the inner levels. Besides, this is a labour of love.

In the first meditation, you make the base and basic landscape – hills, rivers, roads, boundary walls and trees – fashioning the features from a clay-like substance that dries in moments. Close the meditation by painting it.

In the second meditation you make the houses, in the third the farm buildings, and in the fourth the amenities such as a post office and police station. In the fifth, you create the tiny inhabitants, who are convincing characters with distinct personalities. Consider what kind of characters the children would like to see and add types that you, too, would like to see.

Over the course of time, you can return periodically to the village, adding details so that it becomes more real each time. Take pride in your work, and at the close of each meditation carry that care and dedication with you into the real world.

'The first duty of love is to listen.'

Paul Tillich

Creating abundance

Money has no intrinsic value. Cash, cheques and credit cards are just paper and plastic; even stocks and shares change in value from day to day. Yet our attitude to money can reveal much about our personality and our view of what life has to offer. Saving for a rainy day may be financially prudent, but fear of spending money in case there might not be any more to replace it is an expression of a self-destructive tendency arising from a lack of self-worth (see page 108). By treating ourselves, we are exercising a certain degree of power. This increases our self-confidence and affirms our belief that there will be more money to replace what we have spent.

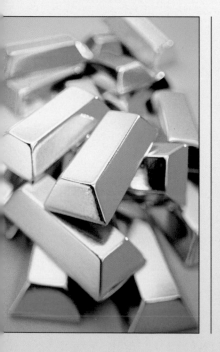

The right to receive

Some of us have trouble with money either because we feel that we do not deserve it or because it forces us to make choices and take on more responsibilities. It may even be that we feel it is wrong to enjoy material prosperity and at the same time practise spirituality. Cultural conditioning has programmed us to believe that the love of money is the root of all evil and that spiritual seekers should be impoverished aesthetes, but there is nothing intrinsically virtuous about being poor. If you are always struggling to make ends meet and worrying about money, you will be constantly diverted from your main purpose in life, which is to realize your true potential.

Ask for what you want and be prepared to accept it when it comes. Whether you want to address your request to God, Jesus, Buddha, the angels or your own unconscious mind, do it in the knowledge that you will receive what is right for you. The simple act of asking gives expression to your often unconscious thoughts and that is enough to focus the mind on attracting what you desire.

'The rain may pour down from the heavens, but, if you only hold up a thimble, a thimbleful is all you receive.'

Ram Dass

Attracting prosperity

By using affirmations during meditation we can identify what is preventing us from accepting our rightful share and reprogramme the unconscious to remove the restrictions. Simply choose one of the sentences below that you feel relates to your current circumstances, memorize it and repeat it as often as you wish during the meditation.

- The creative force of the universe is inexhaustible; there is plenty for everyone.
- I am ready to receive the blessings of this abundant universe.
- Everything I need is coming to me effortlessly right now.
- The creative force always provides.
- Money flows to me in a positive and abundant way right now.

Pause for a minute or so after each repetition, and listen to the spontaneous response. Do not try to influence or analyse what comes through; simply let it flow. At first, it will probably be nonsense, the equivalent of the images in the early stages of sleep before we sink into deeper states of consciousness. If you stick with it, however, eventually a dialogue will develop in which the truth of your situation and your real attitude to abundance in all its forms will be made known. Prepare to be surprised.

End the meditation by envisaging yourself enjoying the prosperity you seek. When you are ready, return to waking consciousness by counting down from ten to one and becoming once again aware of your body and the surroundings.

Guilt

Guilt is a self-imposed prison from which we must free ourselves. It is the result of trying to live up to a self-image based on unrealistic expectations of life and our capacity to cope with the challenges that give life its purpose. It is the feeling that we should have done things differently in the past – things that cannot now be altered. It is therefore pointless to punish ourselves; unless that suffering opens the heart to compassion – the understanding and self-knowledge that comes from mistakes – and gives us the will to forgive ourselves and move on. The following exercise will create the mind-set that will help you to accept that mistakes make us human, and that, by forgiving ourselves, we can open up to our true nature.

there is no embarrassment in expressing your feelings . . .

The riverbank

Make yourself comfortable, close your eyes and, when you feel fully relaxed, imagine that you are rowing downstream in a small boat on a beautiful summer's day. It seems a shame to make hard work of such an enjoyable journey, so draw up the oars, settle back and let the current carry you along. Take in the view as you drift gently along, and listen to the sound of the lapping water and the birds. Feel the fresh breeze and sunlight on your face.

Soon a cloud covers the sun and you hear the sound of voices on the shore. There you can see the scene that has been causing you to feel guilty. You can

'If you are still being hurt by an event that happened to you at 12, it is the thought that is hurting you now.'

James Hillman

see yourself and the other parties involved and hear what is being said, but this time the distance between you creates a sense of detachment. It is like watching actors playing a scene from your own life. From this objective view, the cause of the misunderstanding will be clear to you and you will feel the need to explain your feelings to the other parties.

At that moment, the scene freezes and everyone is motionless. You can now say whatever you need to get off your chest, and it will be heard by those who need to hear, including your own Higher Self. There is no embarrassment in expressing your feelings, or in saying that you are sorry or that you would act differently if you had the chance again.

Now it is important to affirm that what has happened cannot be changed. However, the experience has not been wasted. You have learnt from this and, because you have done so, the experience will not be repeated.

With this, the sun emerges from behind the cloud and the scene dissolves. You can now continue your journey, carried by the current until you are ready to return to waking consciousness.

Decision-making

Sometimes it is difficult to make significant, life-changing decisions entirely on the basis of rational arguments, even if one option has clear practical advantages. A tempting job offer or a move to a new house may appear to answer our immediate needs; but, if it involves leaving family and friends behind, taking on new responsibilities or a substantial debt, we may experience nagging doubts that will affect our judgement. In such cases, it is not always possible to trust entirely to intuition, as it may simply be anxiety or fear of change that makes it difficult to commit ourselves. If you find that you are unable to make a decision because your emotions are clouding your judgement, try the following exercise to clarify your thinking and explore the potential problems of each path. (See also 'Seeking guidance' on page 104, 'The Akashic library' exercise on page 106 and the appropriate pathworking visualization on pages 112–119.)

Choosing the right path

If you have to choose between two alternatives, pick one and visualize yourself progressing along that particular path. Imagine what might happen if you commit yourself to this course and be aware of how you feel during this inner journey.

Visualize a typical day in your new job or your new house. Do you have a sense of satisfaction and security? What are the primary advantages and problems of this path? Are the difficulties as insurmountable as you had feared, or can they be solved, reduced or evaded? Put the anxieties and doubts that you had into perspective by facing them in your imagination.

What could you learn if the path is a difficult one? Neither option will be problem-free, or there would be no purpose in the experience, but one should feel 'right' for you and offer the greater challenge.

Now commit yourself mentally to the second path, and follow that through in the same way.

Once you have made your decision, stick with it. All paths ultimately lead to the same end – the fulfilment of your potential; but, if you constantly change your mind, you drain yourself of the vital energy that will see you through the journey.

Be your own oracle

'What you are is what you have done, what you will be is what you do now.'

Buddha

This supplementary exercise for seeking inner guidance can be fun, as well as potentially very helpful in revealing what we really feel about the choices we have to make. This exercise can be very beneficial in developing your powers of visualization and intuition.

When you are relaxed, imagine you are in a torch-lit hallway of a house. The house is a symbol of your psyche. Its furnishings and general condition will reveal much about your state of mind if you choose to analyse them. Now you have to make a choice. You are faced with a number of doors, one for each possible course of action in your present dilemma.

On the outside of each door is a picture representing one of those possibilities. Pass through the door and observe whatever is to be found there, but do so with objectivity. You may see yourself in your new situation as if you are watching a movie, or you may find that the room is a symbolic representation of your attitude to the dilemma you are faced with. When you are ready, leave the room and see what lies behind each of the other doors. In this way, you can explore all of your choices.

When you come out of the meditation, write down everything you can remember about your feelings and the imagery. You can then consult a reliable dictionary of symbols or trust to your common sense and intuition to reveal the truth of what you have seen.

Setting your sights on success

One of the most effective methods of transforming your life and making your dreams come true is a form of meditation known as creative visualization. This ancient esoteric discipline for harnessing mental energy is now widely practised by psychotherapists, personal growth gurus and spiritual seekers of all persuasions, and was proved to be effective by Carl Jung, the father of modern psychoanalysis, who renamed it 'active imagination'. By utilizing the power of our imagination, enforced with positive affirmations, we can identify our goals and manifest positive changes in whichever areas of our life that we wish to improve. Creative visualization is distinct from positive thinking in that it uses the power of thought to create an alternative reality on an inner level, which serves as a blueprint for whatever we wish to give form to in the physical dimension. To prove its effectiveness for yourself, try the following meditations.

Short-term goals

Decide on something that you can easily attain within a week. It should be something that is both practical and possible; otherwise you risk inner resistance. It could be something you would like to buy but cannot afford at the moment, a situation such as meeting a new friend or partner, or even a promotion at work.

Now relax into your meditation and envisage yourself having attained whatever it is that you desire, in as much detail as possible. It is important to accept this scene as a reality that is manifesting at this very moment on an inner level and will shortly influence events in the physical. You are not merely wishing for something, but creating it.

you are not merely wishing for something, but creating it . . .

Finally, affirm in words of your own choosing that this will happen within a week and thank the universe, your guardian angel, God or your own Higher Self for supplying it.

Long-term goals

'If you move toward your goals, expressing all your power, opportunity will find you as a result of your actions.'

Stuart Wilde

If you wish to create fundamental changes in your life in the long term, you have to be less definite about the details, so that you will be able to accept what is right for you rather than what you desire. For example, you may be experiencing difficulties with relationships because you keep falling for the 'wrong' person. If you meditate on meeting the person who is right for you, regardless of whether they conform to your ideals, then you will open yourself to other possibilities and maybe subsequently attract someone who will enrich your life.

Now decide upon your long-term goal. This time it should be something that will bring you happiness and that offers the opportunity for personal growth rather than temporary gratification. It must also be for the benefit of all concerned. Therefore, it is no use visualizing a promotion that comes at the cost of someone more deserving, or a new partner whose arrival involves heartbreak for their present partner.

Perhaps you want a stable relationship, a well-paid, satisfying job, a happy home and family. Whatever you want, visualize your ideal scene, but try to avoid putting faces to the people involved. Keep them anonymous, and do not fill in too many details; otherwise you risk putting limitations on your gifts. Feel happy with what you see and enjoy it – after all, that is the purpose of the exercise, not just acquiring more possessions or a more affluent lifestyle. Resist the temptation to manipulate the images, and let them arise spontaneously.

Finally, affirm that this scene is being created right now in the inner levels, and will manifest for the highest good of all concerned at some point in the near future when it is right for it to do so.

Increasing your creativity

The key to creativity, whether it is writing, painting, sculpture or any other form of self-expression, is inspiration. Once we have an idea, giving it form is merely a matter of honing the skills we have acquired until we have transformed our vision into something we can share with others. 'Genius,' as Thomas Edison once said, 'is one per cent inspiration and ninety-nine per cent perspiration.' Yet how do we catch that elusive, intangible thought that we need to get our creative juices flowing? Meditation offers one of the most effective ways of making ourselves receptive to inspiration by opening up a channel to the unconscious and the all-knowing higher self.

'An essential portion of any artist's labour is not creation so much as invocation.'

Lewis Hyde

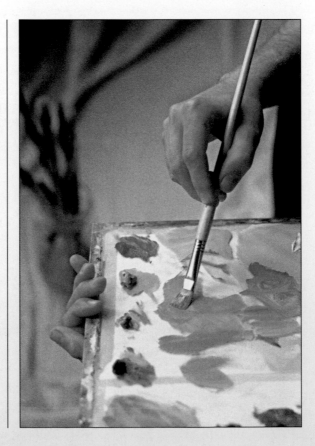

Exploring

When you are sufficiently relaxed, imagine you are standing in the main square of a small town, village or city that you have never visited before, but which is strangely familiar to you. You are not apprehensive but excited at the prospect of exploring this place, because you know that somewhere here is a treasure awaiting discovery.

Before setting off to explore, familiarize yourself with your surroundings. What character does the place have? What period does it represent? Are there signposts that might give you a clue as to where to begin your search? Do you feel drawn in any particular direction or towards a particular building?

When you are ready, begin to explore and let yourself be guided by your intuition. Enjoy the tingle of anticipation you feel as you wander at will through a labyrinth of unexplored alleyways and streets, anticipating a new discovery at every turn.

Do not impose any expectations upon yourself, and do not be disappointed if you do not uncover anything significant on your first outing; simply enjoy the time off from the intensity of your everyday routine and responsibilities, and know that in time you will uncover more than you could ever have imagined.

A self-portrait

Our own lives and experiences can provide a rich and varied source of material. This is particularly true for writers, but also for composers and artists, and even for anyone who wishes to express their individuality in the decoration of their own home, for example.

To mine this vein of ideas, relax into meditation and recall a scene from your early childhood. Picture the place where you lived or somewhere you visited. Can you fill in significant details, such as the clothes you wore, the friends you played with, the games you played together and the toys you played with? Once you have established the setting and characters, do not be tempted to manipulate the images. Allow the scene to play itself out spontaneously as you watch with detachment.

'As you begin to pay attention to your own stories and what they say about you, you will enter into the exciting process of becoming, as you should be, the author of your own life, the creator of your own possibilities.'

Mandy Aftel
The Story of Your Life

When you come out of the meditation, express what you saw and felt then, and how you feel about it now, in whatever medium you choose. It might form the basis of a short story, a scene in that novel that you have always wanted to write or the picture you have been meaning to paint. Or maybe you want to include something from that time in your home or garden, to act as a conscious reminder of the child that still lives inside you.

Autobiography

'I am still learning.'

Michelangelo

Vary the previous visualization by moving on from that scene to others in your childhood, and then to later years, as you trace the outline of your life, scene by scene, as in an autobiography or film. Take your time and develop each scene in as much detail as you can. This will stimulate a stream of potentially useful imagery from the unconscious, and possibly even uncover suppressed memories that could be blocking the flow of creative energy. It may also reveal any negative attitudes to your own self-expression, picked up unconsciously in your past from parents, teachers or other children, which enforced the idea that you could not do something. Do not make the mistake of thinking that your life is not interesting enough to provide material for an artistic endeavour. There is nothing more interesting than people. Even in the big blockbuster novels and movies it is how people react to events that makes the story come alive, and not the special effects.

the creature symbolizes everything that is holding you back . . .

Exorcising the creativity monster

This visualization is adapted from an exercise devised by the American artist and author Julia Cameron, whose workshops have helped many people to free their own creative spirit.

When you are comfortable and suitably relaxed, imagine that you have before you a doll-sized marionette with movable joints, the type that artists use when

they are studying the human figure. You also have a box of materials with which to decorate the doll and labels with which to make miniature placards to hang around its neck.

You are going to create a creature that symbolizes everything that is holding you back from expressing yourself. If you believe that only the great artists should make art, you could cut out a picture of the face of someone like Picasso and paste it on the doll. If you feel that your creative energies are being sapped by alcohol, tobacco or something else, put that object in the puppet's hand.

When you have finished creating the puppet in your imagination, take a handful of labels and write on each a negative phrase that sums up your attitude to your art; for example, 'I'm not good enough', 'It's too late' or 'Why bother?'

Finally, face your inner creative monster and affirm that you are done with its nagging and draining of your creative spirit. Now set fire to it in your mind, and watch with great satisfaction as it burns.

4 Soul searching

Seeking guidance from your higher self

It would be wonderful to know that in difficult times we could turn to a close, compassionate and loyal friend, from whom we could seek comfort and impartial advice – a teacher, guru, personal counsellor and protective parent all in one. Such a person is a rarity in the real world, but they do exist within each of us, and are available for consultation and consolation 24 hours a day. Some people refer to this all-knowing essence as the Higher Self, soul, spirit, guide or guardian angel, while those of a more scientific mind might call it the unconscious. Whatever name you use, it has all the answers you seek. To open this channel of communication, all you need to do is ask for help in any of the following ways.

Treasure hunt

This exercise encourages you to trust your intuition, which is the first step in establishing communication with the Higher Self.

Think of a personal object that you have lost or misplaced recently, such as a book, key or watch. Then enter a meditative state and concentrate on that object. Picture yourself holding it, then see it disappear. Now in your mind search your home from room to room, while asking your inner guide to reveal where it can be found. Do not allow your rational mind to interfere and discount possible hiding places. Remain open and confident. Expect to be drawn to the place where you will find it, and when you come out of meditation look there.

It may take quite a bit of practice to develop this talent, but in time you will be able to enter the necessary state of heightened awareness as you search.

The counsellor

If you need an answer to a specific question, or general guidance, you can ask your Higher Self in person (see also the relevant pathworking visualization on pages 112–119). When you are comfortable and suitably relaxed, enter your inner sanctuary using the visualization on page 106.

Once inside, you may find that your guide is already there waiting for you, as it is invariably the unconscious that prompts you to make contact. If not, focus on a shadowy corner of your chosen sacred place and ask your guide to appear. Imagine them stepping out of the shadows or emerging from a blinding light. If you experience difficulties visualizing, you can use a familiar figure such as Jesus, Buddha or someone you admire as a focus. The significant element is the message, not the messenger; their appearance is purely symbolic. You may not receive a clear image of your guide until you have broken down any resistance to the idea from the doubting ego. Instead, you may feel their presence, or hear that still, small voice within.

When you have contact, phrase your question as you would an affirmation – that is, in simple terms avoiding ambiguity. Do not be discouraged if you do not receive an answer immediately. It is quite common to receive an answer in your dreams when the conscious, rational mind is sleeping.

'What lies behind us and what lies before us are small matters compared with what lies within us.'

Ralph Waldo Emerson

the significant element is the message, not the messenger . . .

Creating an inner sanctuary

There are times when we need to take a break from the pressures of modern living and make space just for ourselves, but we cannot always take a holiday or put our lives on hold whenever we want to. However, meditation affords us the opportunity to retire, at a moment's notice, to a place of peace within ourselves, where we can cultivate a sense of detachment, seek guidance or simply gather strength for the day. This inner sanctuary is usually envisaged as a garden, but there are other settings which might be more suitable and productive, depending on your personality and circumstances.

enjoy and take satisfaction from your achievements . . .

The Akashic library

You may find that a library or study is most conducive if you are a student, or if your work is of an intellectual nature. Such a setting can be used to improve your powers of concentration, increase your ability to retain facts and seek inspiration when you need to reflect on something that seems difficult to resolve.

Begin your visualization by imagining you are standing beneath the imposing façade of the world's largest library where every book, magazine and newspaper that has ever been published is stored. Over the massive doors is written the inscription 'Knowledge, wisdom, understanding'.

You enter and follow the sign to the reading room, where you will find a chair and desk reserved in your name. There are no other desks here. You will have the room to yourself for as long as you wish.

You can simply sit and enjoy the silence or you can take a book from the thousands of volumes to be found in the bookcases lining the walls. The answers to all your questions are to be found here.

The artist's studio

The purpose of creating an inner sanctuary is to offer yourself an opportunity to withdraw from the world temporarily and seek serenity in the silence. If you are a creative person and choose to envisage an artist's studio, it should be to admire and draw satisfaction from your own work that you find there, rather than seeking inspiration. So picture your ideal studio or gallery, but furnish it with your finished work rather than blank canvases.

It is important to enjoy, value and take satisfaction from your achievements and, if you do, this will help to nurture new ideas.

> 'Abide at the centre of your being, for the more you leave it the less you learn.'
>
> Lao Tzu

The walled garden

If your inner sanctuary is a garden, you will see it take shape with each successive meditation.

Do not be surprised, however, if you find it in a neglected state on your first visit. This indicates that there is much work to be done on the inner level, to clear confusion and clarify your thoughts. So start with a symbolic renovation in the garden itself. See yourself pulling up the weeds, pruning the dead wood, cutting the grass, sweeping the paths and restoring the water features and garden furniture. This is not work – it is an effortless labour of love.

When your work is done, listen to the sound of birdsong, the drone of insects and the gentle breeze through the trees. Smell the scent of the cut grass and the intoxicating perfume of the flowers. Enjoy the tranquillity that you have created, until you are ready to return to the outside world.

Clearing negative conditioning

As children, we are conditioned to accept the idea that good behaviour should be rewarded and bad deeds must be punished. The real world, however, is not governed by such laws – we make our own good fortune, which is directly related to our sense of self-worth. Most of us undervalue ourselves, because we feel that we do not live up to our own ideals. Consequently, our income, our relationships and our quality of life is seldom better than what we believe we deserve. If our self-image is low, we may even undermine our chances of success by unconsciously sabotaging any opportunities that arise to improve ourselves and our circumstances – although most of us settle for putting limitations on our good fortune by telling ourselves that it cannot last. The following exercise is designed to overcome this impulse by recasting what some might call our conscience as a guide or mentor.

expressing your anxieties is half the battle · · ·

Meeting your inner guide

> 'Be gentle with yourself. If you will not be your own unconditional friend, who will be? If you are playing an opponent and you are also opposing yourself – you are going to be outnumbered.'
>
> Dan Millman
> *Everyday Enlightenment*

Relax into meditation by focusing on the breath. Then, when you are ready, imagine a small, white dot in the distance. Hold this image for as long as you can. It may be more difficult than you might think, but with practice it will become easier.

After a minute or two, see the dot drawing nearer, revealing itself to be a swirling vapour, out of which steps a familiar figure. This could be a person from history whom you respect, a spiritual leader, a teacher, a friend or a family figure. It should be someone whom you admire for their wisdom and compassion, someone you imagine would listen before offering impartial advice – not a person who would judge you. If you cannot think of a real person, visualize an anonymous figure on to whom you can project these qualities.

Now express your fears and own up to what you consider to be your 'mistakes'. Expressing your anxieties in this way is half the battle towards exorcising them, and if you can laugh at the more ridiculous worries you have indulged in so much the better.

Now recall the love you have shared with other people, the sacrifices you have made and the dues you have paid in one form or another during your lifetime. You have worked and studied as hard as anyone else, perhaps even more so. Have you not already made amends for whatever transgressions and mistakes you made, or imagine that you made?

Now share your hopes and aspirations with your mentor and ask for guidance.

Do not be surprised if you receive practical advice such as treating yourself to something you can afford but would normally deny yourself, or doing something on impulse (within reason). When such ideas pop into your head, it is invariably the Higher Self prompting you to loosen up; and, in so doing, act on faith, expecting your cup to be filled as soon as you have emptied it.

Working with archetypes

You can safely explore the various aspects of your own psyche by meditating on the divine attributes described in the Kabbalah, the Jewish mystical teaching that forms the foundation of the western esoteric tradition. From a psychological viewpoint, they can be seen as representing the various complementary aspects of the persona that need to be integrated if we are to achieve wholeness; on a spiritual level, they can be interpreted as symbolic of the stages that we all need to pass through on our ascent to self-realization and perfection.

Archetypes and the anatomy of the psyche

> 'We are each a diamond of many facets and flaws.'
>
> Dan Millman
> *Everyday Enlightenment*

Malkhut (The Kingdom) – the naked form of a strong, healthy man or woman representing the physical world.

Yesod (The Foundation) – an ambitious prince or gifted and wilful child representing the ego.

Hod (Reverberation) – a receptive and enthusiastic student representing the active aspect of our natural intelligence which is concerned with communication and learning.

Nezah (Eternity) – a sensual figure representing the instincts and the preoccupation with pleasure and pain.

Tiferet (Beauty) – an angel representing the Higher Self.

Gevurah (Judgement) – a learned authority figure representing self-discipline, decisiveness and discernment.

Hesed (Mercy) – a maternal figure representing tolerance, unconditional love and forgiveness.

Daat (Higher Knowledge) – a composer or artist deep in thought representing inspiration and intuition. This is not strictly an archetype, but rather a hidden attribute, a chasm we have to cross from worldly awareness to enlightenment.

Binah (Understanding) – a learned, compassionate and patient teacher whose uncommon understanding is the result of long study and reflection.

Hokhmah (Wisdom) – a prophet or mystic whose glimpse of the greater reality represents revelation.

Keter (The Crown) – the sun or a radiant star representing the divine aspect of human nature.

To use these symbols in meditation, you will need to make a pack of illustrated cards, one for each archetype. You could draw them yourself, or cut out suitable images that fit the descriptions from books and magazines. Stick each one on to a stiff card, slightly larger than a normal playing card.

If, for example, you want to bring a particular quality to the fore, just pick the appropriate card and fix it in your mind. Then close your eyes and take several deep breaths. When you feel suitably relaxed, focus on the image and allow yourself to enter the picture.

The shadow self

If we are to be fully integrated and balanced human beings, we need to acknowledge and assimilate the shadow side of our nature, the flawed aspects that we would deny and disown in the mistaken belief that they are negative or inappropriate and therefore bad. Yet, in denying the existence of these complementary qualities, we risk diminishing our authenticity and are less able to deal with challenging situations. This inflexibility creates conflicts in personal relationships, in society and between nations, but it is relatively simple to resolve such difficulties.

The next time you experience friction between yourself and another person, try to take a more balanced perspective by reflecting on your shadow in the following way.

Relax into meditation and picture the person with whom you are in conflict. Now ask yourself three questions: 'What have I received from X?', 'What have I given to X?' and 'What difficulties have I caused X?'

In reflecting on these questions at length in the calm detachment and heightened awareness of meditation, you will see that your bruised ego has been highly selective in sifting through the evidence in your favour.

'No one can become conscious of the shadow without considerable moral effort . . . it involves recognizing the dark aspects of the personality as present and real.'

Carl Jung

Pathworking

One of the most revealing methods for increasing self-awareness is the arcane technique known as pathworking, which involves meditating on a specific aspect of the personality within a symbolic landscape. If you require an answer to a specific question, or if you want to explore a particular aspect of your personality, you can access the relevant level of consciousness by exploring the corresponding area in this symbolic map of the psyche. If, for example, you feel the need to be more confident and assertive, you will need to visualize the Court of Judgement, which is presided over by the archetype representing the qualities of self-discipline, decisiveness and discernment. The appearance of the relevant archetype is a sign that you have entered the desired region of the unconscious. Alternatively, you can wander at will through this inner world to experience the different qualities and bring them into your everyday consciousness.

The inner journey

Begin by making yourself comfortable, closing your eyes and establishing a regular rhythm of breathing.

Visualize yourself standing outside a house, the size, décor and state of repair of which is symbolic of your current state of mind. Observe as much detail as you can before you enter, but do not be tempted to analyse anything until after you return to waking consciousness.

Now explore one of the following eleven aspects, depending on your needs.

'Pathworkings are doorways between the known and the physical and the unknown and the non-corporeal. They accomplish their work through the medium of creative imagination . . . They can and do cause actual physical effects in the everyday world.'

Dolores Ashcroft-Nowicki
The Shining Paths

Malkhut (The Kingdom)

Contemplate this aspect if you need to be more practical and grounded.

Push open the gate and walk up the path, where you find a strong, healthy young man or woman working in the grounds. They greet you and ask what plans you have for the garden. They will do the digging, pruning, cultivating and landscaping, but you have to give them an outline of your plans and the motivation to do the physical labour.

As you watch them work, you become aware that the human body is a microcosm, a world in miniature containing all the elements that exist in nature and in the universe (the macrocosm). The element of earth is represented by the solidity of our bones, the element of water by the fluidity of our blood, the element of air by our breath and the element of fire by the heat in our skin.

Now consider the mineral element in your bones, which appear solid but are continually growing, and the basic minerals that maintain the vital chemical balance in the body. Then consider the vegetable principle which governs growth and regeneration of the cells. Now become aware of the animal principle – your vitality, curiosity, instinct, sociability and mobility. Finally, become aware of your human attributes – your imagination, inventiveness, memory, reflection and your ability to expand your consciousness and awareness.

113

Yesod (The Foundation)

Contemplate this aspect if you want to become less self-centred and less dependent on people and possessions.

Enter the house, where you will find a child playing in the hall. The child takes delight in showing off an entire town that they have constructed from multicoloured building blocks; but, when you look as if you are losing interest, they destroy it in an attempt to win back your attention.

Alternatively, visualize an ambitious and vain young man who acts as your guide around the lower levels of the house. In each room, he covets every object he shows you and boasts of the cunning means by which he acquired them.

Hod (Reverberation)

Contemplate this aspect to increase your concentration, improve your memory and be more receptive to new ideas.

Enter the study through one of the doors in the hallway, where you will find an enthusiastic young student who is eager to learn whatever you can tell them of the outside world. You engage in a discussion that draws on your practical knowledge of how things work and on the student's theoretical knowledge. Listen carefully to their explanations and let their enthusiasm inspire you. If there is something that you have always wanted to learn about, take encouragement from what you find here.

Everything you have always wanted to know is waiting to be discovered. Do not underestimate your innate capacity to recall facts and communicate ideas. Everything that you have learnt and experienced has left its indelible impression in the mind and can be recalled at any time. You only have to enter this study to recollect it.

Nezah (Eternity)

Contemplate this aspect of the psyche when you need to get in touch with your sensual nature. Meditating on this aspect can be particularly helpful if you need to resolve guilt issues concerning your sexuality or if you feel too self-conscious or awkward in company.

Visualize yourself in a pleasure garden with long, tree-lined walks, ornamental fountains, statues and an elaborate maze. Do you risk entering the maze? If so, what do you find there?

As you wander through the grounds, sniff each scented rosebush and savour the smell of freshly cut grass. Now stroll into the orchard and pick a peach from a tree laden with ripe fruit. Feel the texture of the fruit as you turn it over in your hand before biting into its juicy flesh. When you have satisfied your appetite, you find that your attention is drawn to another part of the garden, where you can hear the faint strains of beautiful music mingling with the sound of bubbling water in the fountains and the sweet chirping of birdsong. Enter this secluded part of the estate, and indulge yourself in the pleasures on offer. You might find yourself at a grand picnic with music and dancing, or invited to join in frivolous games. Can you join in or do you feel too self-conscious?

what do you find there?

115

Tiferet (Beauty)

Contemplate this aspect when you need guidance or comfort.

Visualize yourself in your inner sanctuary. It might be a traditional place of worship, a walled garden, a deserted beach, a forest or even a mountaintop. The location is not important. It is your own personal sacred space, somewhere that offers you peace of mind and a sense of security. Enter a state of deep relaxation and simply ask that your guide, guardian angel or Higher Self appear. Know that, whatever form it takes, it is an aspect of your own personality and that you have this all-knowing supreme being within you for you to call upon at any time you choose.

your own personal sacred space offers you peace of mind . . .

Gevurah (Judgement)

Contemplate this aspect when you need to be decisive.

Imagine you are a judge weighing the evidence in a case that is strikingly similar to one that occupies you at the moment in the 'real world'. You view the evidence and hear the arguments from both sides with impartiality then retire to the solitude of your room to contemplate the verdict.

Alternatively, visualize yourself as a loving parent who must decide on the best course of action in a dispute between two of your children, the dispute being a problem that you need to resolve in 'real life'.

Hesed (Mercy)

Contemplate this aspect when you need to practise tolerance, compassion and forgiveness, or if you believe you are being too self-critical.

Visualize a maternal figure who can offer unconditional love, and unburden yourself of any feelings of guilt, anger, envy or whatever needs to be cleared, in the certainty that you will be forgiven by her.

Alternatively, imagine your own child coming to you in a highly emotional state regarding something they have done that is actually quite trivial. You take them in your arms and comfort them.

Remember what it was like to be a child and how acutely you felt every injustice and harsh word. Affirm that you will treat every individual you meet with compassion, as someone who is still learning through experience. Remember also that you yourself are still learning and resolve to be as forgiving of your own mistakes.

Daat (Higher Knowledge)

Contemplate this hidden attribute when you are seeking inspiration or wish to develop your intuition.

Visualize yourself in an artist's studio, standing before a blank canvas. An image will appear spontaneously on the paper, and all you have to do is stay focused on it as it changes. Do not try to analyse or manipulate the image in any way; just let it unfold. It is likely that the breakthrough into this dimension will be marked by the appearance of a single eye that appears to be staring back at you. This can be quite startling if you are not expecting it. Do not be afraid, however. It signifies the opening of your own Third Eye Chakra and the capacity for psychic insight.

Binah (Understanding)

Contemplate this aspect when you are looking for insight into a particular problem, or to understand the significance of a difficult situation.

Imagine you have the opportunity to consult an educated and erudite specialist in a subject that interests you. It could be an academic, a skilled craftsman, a qualified professional, a medical expert or a religious authority. Visit them in their natural environment and sense the tradition of knowledge, training and skill that lies behind their expertise.

Hokhmah (Wisdom)

Contemplate this aspect when you seek enlightenment or need to experience a deep sense of peace.

Imagine you are having a private audience with a guru, philosopher or spiritual teacher in a setting that lends itself to quiet reflection. Become aware of the aura of stillness and serenity that emanates from their presence as they answer

your questions with infinite patience. After some time, you are overwhelmed by their unconditional love for humanity and generosity of spirit, and find yourself becoming one with your teacher. You look out through their eyes, and perceive the greater reality that lies beyond the physical world. You are now acutely aware of the unity of all things, and your own place and purpose in existence.

Keter (The Crown)

Contemplate this aspect when you wish to tune into the divine aspect of your nature, for healing or detachment.

Visualize yourself at the entrance to a long tunnel, at the end of which is an intense, white light. As you approach the light, you sense the presence of divine beings. These angels or highly evolved spiritual entities invite you to join them. You enter a realm of pure consciousness and experience the inexpressible beauty and perfection of the divine.

119

Glimpsing a greater reality

Many of our problems are of our own making – the result of the way we perceive the world. We find it difficult to believe in anything beyond the physical dimension, because our senses tell us that if we cannot see it, touch it, taste it or smell it, then it does not exist. It is not 'real'. As the Buddhists and followers of other esoteric traditions would tell us, however, consciousness is the only reality. The physical world is an illusion. Nothing is solid. Our physical world is given the illusion of form by the speed at which particles of matter move in space and by the distance between those particles. When we learn to raise our consciousness to the realms beyond the material world, we can glimpse a greater reality and ultimately appreciate a pattern and purpose to existence.

'In every human being there slumber faculties by means of which he can acquire for himself knowledge of higher worlds.'

Rudolf Steiner

The hierarchy of existence

This exercise has been practised with minor variations by initiates of the western esoteric tradition for more than 2,000 years. Although it appears comparatively simple, it is potentially extremely powerful and should not be undertaken by anyone with mental or emotional problems, or those under the influence of drugs. Owing to the length and amount of detail, it may be a good idea to record the text at a very leisurely pace, and with sufficient pauses to allow the imagery to take form, and to give yourself time to experience each level of consciousness as you play it back.

When you are suitably relaxed, visualize yourself standing at the edge of the ocean with the waves lapping gently at your feet. You are free of physical sensations. It is your spirit, your consciousness, that is being projected. Now wade out into the depths and swim with the fish. Go deeper into the abyss where the sunlight cannot penetrate; then deeper still, to where the basic matter of life bubbles up from the centre of the earth and mountains in the making are seen in molten form. Now begin your ascent past the myriad forms of aquatic life back to the sparkling sunlight on the surface.

You emerge. Before your feet can touch the sand, however, you begin to rise above the beach and float, as light as a bubble, into the sky. Observe the villages, towns and cities and their inhabitants contributing their experience of life to the group soul. See the newly born, the young, the middle-aged, the elderly and those who are ready to return to the realm of spirit. Look down on the turning earth below, which is teeming with life, nourished by the blue waters of the oceans, rivers, lakes and streams and by the warmth of the sun.

Now ascend through the vastness of space to a point of light beyond the last star. As you approach it, you can see that it is in fact a tunnel of light illuminated by innumerable celestial beings. Beyond is the world of pure spirit, where the evolved souls who have broken free of the wheel of life, death and rebirth are to be found. Linger here as long as you wish. Ask for guidance, healing or the clearing of karmic debt (see 'Karma' in the Glossary, page 123). Most of all, enjoy the tranquillity and heightened awareness at this level of consciousness.

When you are ready, begin your descent though the tunnel of light and back through space until you are hovering over the earth. Open your eyes.

Glossary

Affirmation A positive assertion made while in a meditative state.

Aura A multicoloured radiance of etheric energy surrounding all living creatures, which can be 'seen' by psychics or sensitives and 'read' as indicators of an individual's mental, physical and emotional state/health.

Chakras Vortices of etheric energy in the subtle or astral body located along the spinal column, which absorb and distribute the universal life force through the body. There are thought to be many minor chakras, but only seven major ones. The *Root Chakra* at the base of the spine is the source of kundalini, the 'serpent power', which when released rises up the spine to the brain to stimulate the Crown Chakra, bringing enlightenment. The *Sacral Chakra* is located at the genitals and governs reproduction and sexual energy. The *Solar Plexus Chakra* is located above the navel and is considered the centre of the emotions. On a physical level it governs the digestion and liver. The *Heart Chakra* is found in the centre of the chest and is concerned with the circulation. When stimulated, it becomes a focus for compassion and unconditional love. The *Throat Chakra* governs communication and self-expression. The *Brow Chakra*, also known as the Third Eye Chakra, governs the pineal and pituitary glands. It is found in the centre of the forehead and is concerned with psychic sensitivity, intuition and imagination. The *Crown Chakra* is located at the top of the head and is concerned with enlightenment and the channelling of the universal life force.

Chi The Chinese term for the universal life force.

Creative visualization Meditation exercises which utilize the imagination to imprint an image on the unconscious. Also known as 'active imagination'.

Diaphragm The dome-shaped muscular membrane that separates the abdominal and thoracic cavities.

Dis-ease A state of imbalance in the psyche which manifests in physical symptoms.

Ego The Lower Self, or conscious mind, which is concerned with the physical dimension, as opposed to the Higher Self, or unconscious mind, which is concerned with spiritual awareness. Also known as the Inner Child.

Elements The four fundamental substances (fire, air, water and earth) that constitute everything that is manifest in the universe, and which are symbolic of the constituent aspects (spiritual, mental, emotional and physical) of every individual.

Grounding The act of focusing energy in the physical realm.

Heart Centre Also known as the Heart Chakra, this is concerned with compassion and unconditional love.

Higher Self The immortal, all-knowing, multifaceted aspect of each individual, also known as the soul, spirit or over-soul.

Holistic An approach to healing which involves considering the person as a whole, multidimensional being (existing in the spiritual, mental, emotional and physical dimensions simultaneously), rather than concentrating exclusively on the physical aspect and symptoms.

Inner Child Another name for the ego, used by esoteric groups, personal growth gurus and complementary therapists to denote the innocent aspect of the personality.

Karma The law of cause and effect, according to Hindu tradition. Every action results in a reaction. If someone wrongs another person, they will have to pay for it in this life or the next. Contrary to popular belief, however, they will be prompted to 'repay' the debt by their own conscience, rather than through the intervention of a god.

Life force See Universal life force.

Meridians A network of vein-like channels of etheric energy in the subtle body connecting the chakras to the vital organs.

Pathworking The act of expanding awareness into non-physical dimensions using the imagination, archetypes and symbolic images during a guided meditation.

Positive thinking A self-help technique using constructive phrases to alter the individual's perception of themselves and create a receptive attitude.

Prana Hindu term for the universal life force, roughly translating as 'the breath of life'.

Psyche Psychoanalytical term for the essence of the human personality.

Psychosomatic Describes a physical illness that is believed to have its origins in the mind rather than being the result of a biological breakdown.

Self-hypnosis Therapeutic technique for reprogramming the unconscious mind with positive imagery or attitudes to alleviate deep-rooted fears or to clear negative conditioning.

Solar plexus The pit of the stomach beneath the diaphragm.

Universal life force The vital or creative force that sustains all life on Earth. It is variously known as 'chi' in the Chinese tradition, 'prana' in Hinduism and 'bioenergy' in western science.

Visualization See Creative visualization.

Waking consciousness Our normal, everyday awareness of the physical dimension.

Index

Index

Acknowledgements

California Institute of Technology and Carnegie Institution of Washington 120
Corbis UK Ltd/Sheldan Collins 118
    /Philip Harvey 40
    /Gail Mooney 95
Getty Telegraph 6, 63, 64, 65, 72, 78, 113, 119
Octopus Publishing Group Limited/Mark Bolton/'Gardens of Life' designers:
    Elaine Munro and Anthony Hen, RHS Hampton Court 2001 54
    /Colin Bowling 38
    /Peter Pugh-Cook 33 left, 88, 114, 117
    /Jerry Harpur 103
    /Peter Myers 16
    /Gareth Sambridge 51
    /Ian Wallace 9, 14, 21, 41
    /Mark Winwood 11, 18, 45, 47, 48, 67
Hulton Getty 33 right, 53
Getty Image Bank 2, 19, 20, 26, 27, 35, 37, 42, 56, 58, 70, 75, 81, 84, 115
Photodisc 87, 98, 104
Science Photo Library 22
    /Adam Hart-Davis 68
    /Erich Schremp 59
Getty Stone 12, 25, 29, 31, 52, 60, 74, 76, 80, 82, 83, 85, 90, 91, 93, 96,
    101, 107, 108, 110, 116

Executive Editor Jane McIntosh
Editor Rachel Lawrence
Executive Art Editor Peter Burt
Designer Rita Wuthrich
Picture Researcher Christine Junemann
Production Controller Edward Carter
Index compiled by Indexing Specialists